# THE TRUTH
# ABOUT THE
# KU KLUX KLAN

# THE TRUTH ABOUT THE KU KLUX KLAN

## MILTON MELTZER

FRANKLIN WATTS
NEW YORK / LONDON / TORONTO / SYDNEY
1982

A GROLIER COMPANY

Photographs courtesy of:
The Schomberg Center for Research in Black Culture,
New York Public Library: p. 7;
Culver Pictures: pp. 25, 32, 48;
United Press International:
pp. 41, 69, 91, 96, 105.

Library of Congress Cataloging in Publication Data

Meltzer, Milton.
The truth about the Ku Klux Klan.

Bibliography: p.
Includes index.
Summary: Discusses the emergence of the Ku Klux Klan
during Reconstruction, its rebirth during the 1920's
and 1960's, Klan activity today, who joins it and why,
and what can be done about it.
1. Ku Klux Klan (1915-   )—History—
Juvenile literature. 2. Ku Klux Klan—
History—Juvenile literature.
3. Terrorism—United States—
History—Juvenile literature.
[1. Ku Klux Klan—History] I. Title.
HS2330.K63M44   1982      322.4'2'0973      82-8532
ISBN 0-531-04498-X                            AACR2

# CONTENTS

# THE TRUTH
# ABOUT THE
# KU KLUX KLAN

# 1

## WHY IS IT REBORN?

It is a hot Sunday morning in the summer of 1980.

A group of Ku Klux Klansmen, armed and uniformed, board a truck in a suburb of Houston, Texas, and drive ten miles to a swampy patch of land above Galveston Bay. It is a fifty-acre camp where once a week the Klansmen train in guerrilla warfare. All day long they practice tactical maneuvers, military drills and agility exercises. In a quonset hut they listen to classroom lectures on guerrilla fighting given by Klan instructors who served in the Vietnam War.

Their goal? To prepare for the day when they can forcibly install a racist government in the United States. "We'll set up our own state here in Texas and announce that all non-whites have twenty-four hours to leave," said Grand Dragon Louis Beam, a camp instructor. "Lots of them won't believe us when we say we'll get rid of them, so we'll have to exterminate a lot of them the first time around."

The Texas Klan's blueprint for a revolution is a book called *The Turner Diaries*. It provides details on explosives, military tactics, supplies, logistics and potential targets for terrorism. It demands that all opponents of racism be hanged.

• It is June 22, 1964. That day three young workers in the campaign to extend civil rights in Mississippi—Michael

Schwerner, 24, James Chaney, 21, and Andrew Goodman, 20,—drive into Neshoba County to investigate the burning of a church, and disappear. Six weeks later, the FBI finds their bodies buried twenty feet deep under Mississippi's red clay. When their murderers are found, they prove to be Ku Klux Klansmen.

• It is October, 1921. The New York *World* publishes a tabulation of acts of violence committed across the nation by the Ku Klux Klan in the past twelve months. The record shows the Klan guilty of four killings, one mutilation, one blinding with acid, forty-one floggings, twenty-seven tar-and-feather parties, five kidnappings, forty-three warnings to leave town, sixteen parades at which threatening placards are carried.

• It is the night of October 29, 1869. Abram Colby, a black member of the Georgia state legislature, is at home with his family. All are asleep when suddenly the door is smashed open and a band of Kluxers run in, take Mr. Colby out of his bed, carry him off to the woods, and whip him for over three hours, leaving him for dead.

Two years later, a congressional committee goes south to investigate Klan violence and terror. They interview hundreds of victims, among them Abram Colby. After he tells them what happened that night, the committee asks him what the Klan raiders said to him:

> A-They said to me, "Do you think you will ever vote another damned radical ticket?" I said, "I will not tell you a lie." I supposed they would kill me anyhow. I said, "If there was an election tomorrow, I would vote the radical ticket." They set in and whipped me a thousand licks more, with sticks and straps that had buckles on the ends of them.

Q-What is the character of the men who were engaged in whipping you?

A-Some are first-class men in our town. One is a lawyer, one a doctor, and some are farmers. They had their pistols and they took me in my night-clothes and carried me from home. They hit me five thousand blows. They told me to take off my shirt. I said, "I never do that for any man." My drawers fell down about my feet and they took hold of them and tripped me up. Then they pulled my shirt up over my head. They said I had voted for Grant and had carried the Negroes against them. About two days before they whipped me they offered me $5,000 to go with them and said they would pay me $2,500 in cash if I would let another man go to the legislature in my place. I told them that I would not do that if they would give me all the county was worth.

The worst thing about the whole matter was this. My mother, wife and daughter were in the same room when they came. My little daughter begged them not to carry me away. They drew up a gun and actually frightened her to death. She never got over it until she died. That was the part that grieves me most.

Q-How long before you recovered from the effects of this treatment?

A-I have never got over it yet. They broke something inside of me. I cannot do any work now, though I always made my living before in the barber-shop, hauling wood, and so forth.

Q-You spoke about being elected in the next legislature?

A-Yes, sir, but they run me off during the election. They swore they would kill me if I stayed. The

Saturday night before the election I went to church.
When I got home they just peppered the house with
shot and bullets.

Q-Did you make a general canvas there last fall?
A-No, sir. I was not allowed to. No man can make a
free speech in my county. I do not believe it can be
done anywhere in Georgia.

Q-You say no man can do it?
A-I mean no Republican, either white or colored.

Violence or the threat of violence.

It was the weapon of the Ku Klux Klan, born more than a
century ago, in the years of Reconstruction immediately after
the Civil War. Again when the Klan was revived during the
1920s. Still again in the 1950s and after, in the renewed struggle
for civil rights. And now today, in the 1980s, when America is
more than ever a multi-racial nation, seeking to solve the
complex problems of building a democratic and decent society.

What is the Ku Klux Klan? Where did it come from? Why
is it reborn time and again?

# 2

## UNDERGROUND ARMY

It began in 1865, with a mysterious name. Six young veterans of the Confederate Army were bored with life in their small town of Pulaski, Tennessee. Looking for excitement, they formed a social club they named the Ku Klux Klan. "Ku Klux" was a twist on the Greek word *kuklos,* meaning circle or band. And "Klan" was probably suggested by the Scottish clans. A good name, they thought, for it was fascinatingly odd, yet memorable because of its rhythmic sound and the alliteration of the KKK.

If the name was strange, why not deepen the mystery with an organization and ritual to match? So they tagged their leader the Grand Cyclops and called their meeting place the Den. They swore their members to absolute secrecy and permitted them to appear in public only in disguise. It was fun to attend fairs and parade about town in their weird costumes— a white mask with holes for eyes and nose, a very high conical cardboard hat which made them look like giants, and a long flowing robe. When the Klansmen were out in public they blew signals on small whistles to communicate with each other, or they talked in a garbled language that seemed to make no sense and concealed their true voices.

For a short while the whole business seemed to be only the kind of harmless fun and foolishness a college fraternity goes in for. But before the first year was up, a sinister change took place. The mysterious nature of the original Klan attracted wide attention and its admirers spread Klans with dizzying speed all over the South. By 1867 there were hundreds of local units in operation in every state from Virginia to Texas. They formed an "Invisible Empire" under the command of Grand Dragon Nathan Bedford Forrest. A famed Confederate cavalry general, he had been a slave trader before the war. Now he owned two big cotton plantations and was building railroads in the South. He claimed a membership of over half a million Klansmen. They were all armed, he told the press, and "opposed to Negro suffrage under any and all circumstances."

Every candidate for Klan membership was asked ten questions. Number 5: "Are you opposed to Negro equality, both social and political?" Number 6: "Are you in favor of a white man's government in this country?"

No secrecy, then, about the Klan's true aim. It was an underground terrorist army rebelling against the government. Its chief object was to maintain or restore white supremacy by any means possible. Years later, the ex-slave Pierce Harper recalled what the Klan had done in his Mississippi county:

> After us colored folks was 'sidered free and turned loose, the Ku Klux broke out. Some colored people started to farming, and gathered the old stock. If they got so they made good money and had a good farm, the Ku Klux would come and murder 'em. The government builded schoolhouses, and the Ku Klux went to work and burned 'em down. They'd go to the jails and take the colored men out and knock their brains out and throw 'em in the river.
>
> There was a colored man they taken, his name was Jim Freeman. They taken him and destroyed his stuff and him 'cause he was making some money. Hung

*Klan raiders attack a black family's home at night.*

him on a tree in his front yard, right in front of his cabin.

There was some colored young men went to the schools they'd opened by the government. Some white woman said someone had stole something of hers, so they put them young men in jail. The Ku Klux went to jail and took 'em out and killed 'em. That happened the second year after the war.

Men you thought was your friend was Ku Kluxers, and you'd deal with 'em in stores in the daytime, and at night they'd come out to your house and kill you.

With the surrender of the Confederate armies in 1865, American slavery had come to an end. Four million blacks were free at last, a freedom paid for heavily with their own blood. The old slaveholding economy of the South was in ruins. The conquered Confederate states were out of the Union, waiting to get back in. What direction would the Old South take? Would it adopt democratic ideas and institutions? Or would it hold fast to its slavery-time beliefs and practices?

Much depended on what the President and Congress would do. There were many plans for the reconstruction of the South. Each President, from Lincoln to Johnson to Grant and Hayes, had his own ideas, and so did many factions in Congress. Other forces outside Washington—merchants and manufacturers, bankers and brokers, planters and farmers, abolitionists and ex-slaveowners—pushed for their own policies.

Lincoln wanted the seceded states to come back into the Union under presidential guidance. His first plan would have kept all blacks from voting or holding office. But just before his murder, he said he now believed blacks had "demonstrated in blood their right to the ballot." Upon Lincoln's death, the Tennessean Andrew Johnson succeeded him in the White House and swiftly granted pardons to many leaders of the

Confederacy. His policy was to let their states back into the Union on very easy terms. He withdrew Federal troops from the South, leaving only a handful there.

The Southern states were told to form their own governments and apply for readmission to the Union. They framed new constitutions and elected officials. But none of them offered the ballot to the blacks. Slavery time was only yesterday, and white southerners—as well as many in the North—still believed that blacks were born inferior. Not only were they unfit to take part in politics then, but they could never be expected to learn how. So the ex-Confederates decided that only whites—the "superior" race—could vote.

Result? In the fall of 1865, only months after the fighting had ended, leading Confederates were elected to office everywhere. The crucial task of reconstructing the South was in *their* hands.

They showed at once what they meant to do. Their states all adopted "Black Codes." In all but name these laws restored the blacks to their old position of slaves. "This is a white man's government," said the new governor of South Carolina, "and intended for white men only." He spoke for all the old slave states.

"Home rule" was what the Southern states had clamored for. And this is what it meant to them. The North would not accept it. The Republicans feared that barring the blacks from politics would make the Democratic Party dominant again in the South and in Congress. Modern businessmen refused to put money into an economy heading back into slavery. The abolitionists were furious at the attempt to destroy an emancipation earned by four terrible years of war.

The ex-slaves demanded that the black codes be revoked. They wanted the right to vote and federal protection from the terrorists who stood in their path. They wanted the same freedom whites enjoyed, with equal rights and equal opportunities. They did not ask for black supremacy. Their goal was simply equality. They wanted land to farm, schools for themselves and their children, work at decent wages. We are not here on God's earth to take care of the white man's needs, they said. We have our own lives to lead, and we want to breathe free.

The radical Republicans in Congress saw the effects of President Johnson's Reconstruction policy and worked out a plan to stop it. Early in 1866 a Congressional committee brought scores of witnesses to Washington. Blacks and whites, people of all points of view, testified to what was going on in the South. The seven hundred pages of printed evidence added up to this: Most Southern whites still hated the Union. Those Southern whites who had opposed secession were treated like traitors. The feelings against the blacks were worse than before the war. The states should not return to the Union until they guaranteed the civil rights of *all* their citizens. It was "madness and lunacy" for the President to hand so much power to the ex-Confederates.

Congress then set about passing bills for a different Reconstruction program. No state could be restored until Congress approved its re-entry. The Freedmen's Bureau was continued. It had been set up near the war's end to provide food, clothing and medical care, to settle the freedmen on abandoned lands, and to help them find work and open schools. And finally, a Civil Rights Bill was passed to guarantee the freedmen equality before the law.

Congress divided the South into five military districts controlled by martial law. It took the vote away from large numbers of rebel whites. It declared that all black men could vote and hold office. And it ordered the rebel states to write new and democratic constitutions.

For black people the right to vote was the heart of Reconstruction. Black voters favored the Republican Party because it was the party that ended slavery and gave them the vote. The other party, the Democrats, had long been the party of the slaveholders.

Now, for the first time in Southern history, blacks joined with whites to write new state constitutions which gave both blacks and poor whites the right to vote. No longer did a man have to own property to be able to vote or hold office. Free public education was declared the right of all. Many other badly needed reforms were adopted. When the state constitutions were finished, each state's citizens had to vote on whether to accept them.

Now the Klan swung into action. It used terror to try to defeat the new constitutions. The raiders beat and shot blacks and whites to scare them out of voting. But the Kluxers failed, and the constitutions were approved. By 1869 all the old slave states were back in the Union. All of them had accepted the Thirteenth, Fourteenth and Fifteenth Amendments, outlawing slavery, making blacks citizens, and giving black men the vote.

It was a tremendous leap forward. Huge numbers of people of both races in the South now, for the first time, held political power. And that was the signal for the Klan and several other secret organizations to combine their terror in an attempt to destroy Radical Reconstruction. It would not be a struggle between massed armies. No one wanted another Civil War. The North hoped it would not have to use troops in great numbers to maintain law and order. Nor did the ex-rebels want head-on clashes that would bring down regular army forces.

So the enemies of Reconstruction resorted to business pressure, to vote-buying, to the lash, the torch and the gun. Anyone who tried to educate the former slaves as to their political rights, who sought to help them vote, or who preached black-white equality, was their target.

# 3

# IN THE NAME OF WHITE SUPREMACY

Violence was deeply imbedded in Southern life. The legal power to punish had been the slaveholder's primary method of control. White men in slavery days used flogging, branding, mutilation and mob violence to maintain white supremacy and enforce segregation. At the heart of the slave system were the town and county patrols which enforced the slave codes. The patrols became a weapon of terror against the enslaved black people. No matter what atrocities they inflicted upon the defenseless slaves, they were immune from prosecution. Almost always the law justified the patrollers' violence in the name of the "security" of the white community. Countless reports testify to the arbitrary and cruel nature of many lashings and killings by patrollers. It was often violence that made no sense except as expression of racism and wanton use of power.

Emancipation did not end that violence. "There wasn't no difference between the patrollers and the KKK that I knows of," said J. T. Tims, an ex-slave of Mississippi. "If they'd catch you they all would whip you."

The Klans were really a restoration of the old patrol system. They acted to enforce the authority of the whites over the blacks. For years they tried to exercise a kind of permanent martial law over the supporters of Reconstruction. By the use of great force they sought to break the will of the blacks and reduce them to a condition of unquestioning obedience.

In Georgia alone, during 1868, there were 336 cases of murder or attempted murder of blacks by the Klan. The Freedmen's Bureau reported hundreds of beatings, the victims lashed 300 to 500 times each. One Bureau agent said that in many counties there was "a deep settled determination to make Georgia a white man's state, hence the merciless persecution of all prominent leaders of the Negroes."

In Mississippi, wrote the historian Vernon L. Wharton, for four years the Klan "rode through the country at night, terrifying, whipping, or murdering whites and Negroes who, for one reason or another, were to them undesirable. It is impossible to estimate the number of Negroes tortured or killed during the time that these various gangs flourished."

Anyone and everyone could end in the hands of the lawless bands. "Roving gangs of terrorists," Wharton went on, "murdered respectable Negro preachers, drove off and killed Negro renters of land, rifled stores and took the lives of Jewish merchants, lynched Negro men, women and children who were accused of vague crimes, and killed or robbed peaceful white citizens."

Each gang of terrorists seemed to operate on its own. There was little or no centralized Klan control. While many groups rode under the Klan banner, others took on different names. But all served the same purpose—to enforce white supremacy. In Alamance County of North Carolina, many of the terrorists called themselves the White Brotherhood. After the fall election of 1868, they threw hundreds of black families out of their homes and work for having dared to vote. They gave Joseph Harvey one hundred and fifty lashes on his bare back and clubbed his baby to death. They feared no punishment: the county sheriff, his deputies, and the county's representatives in the state legislature were all in the Brother-hood.

Most of the Klan leaders throughout the South were in the upper ranks of white society. Their followers came from every class, from the sons of wealthy planters to illiterate poor whites. The men who gave the orders were planters, lawyers, editors, doctors, local and state officials. As the whippings and killings spread, these "men of affairs" often denied any responsibility for them. It was "unworthy elements" who had crept into the Klan, taken control and given it a bad name, they said. But no one took that story seriously. "As between the upper and lower classes," wrote Allen W. Trelease, historian of the Klan, "it would be difficult to assign the greater guilt for the atrocities which took place in the name of white supremacy."

With such high backing, local Klans had little to fear. They relied on secrecy, of course, but their main protection was their friends in high places. If their disguises were penetrated, and they were identified, they still suffered no penalties. Other Klansmen gave them false alibis, intimidated witnesses and officials, and manipulated juries. Few were indicted, almost none were convicted.

In Alamance, Alonzo B. Corliss, a white northerner, partially crippled, taught a Quaker-supported black school and headed a political club of black and white Republicans. The Klan raided his home, dragged him into the woods, and gave him thirty lashes. They shaved one side of his head, painted it black, and warned him to leave the county. When he stub-bornly stayed on, his landlord evicted him from his house and no one else would take him in. Corliss had four of the raiders arrested but the law refused to prosecute them.

Often the Kluxers would go on a night raid as though it were a lark, to whip Republicans wherever they found them. One night the hooded riders attacked a black's home where a party was going on. They broke open the door, shot into the house, rushed in and knocked down a woman with a baby in her arms. When the infant fell to the floor, several Klansmen stamped on it. (The child died in a week.) Then they dragged three men outside and lashed them.

It was common for whites who wanted a black farmer's land to organize a Klan raid and drive the family out. If a black took political leadership, they got rid of him. Wyatt Outlaw, the foremost black in Alamance County, was dragged out of his house by twenty Klansmen one night and carried to the town square. They hung him from a tree in front of the courthouse. No one dared try to stop them. The sheriff never left his seat to look for the guilty men, and the case was closed.

In every state of the South the Klan held public schooling to be one of the greatest sins. But the blacks had made it the goal they insisted upon more than anything else. At the time of emancipation, illiteracy among the Southern blacks was over 95 percent. For whites, too, there was no public education system except in North Carolina. As soon as the Union armies took control of Confederate territory, abolitionists and missionaries began to offer education to the blacks. And the freed people themselves started their own schools. Eager pupils of all ages crowded into the classrooms. To the black students, schools and reading and writing were the symbols of freedom. They saw education as their guarantee against the return of slavery.

Southern whites had never believed in education for blacks. When it came, they fought it bitterly. Carpenters refused to build schools, lumber dealers refused to supply wood. Women—white or black—who ventured to teach the ex-slaves were contemptuously called "nigger teacher" and "prostitute." Beyond the insults were other pressures: stores denied the teachers credit, most white homes refused to rent them rooms.

Then came violence. Black pupils were stoned in the schoolyard or on the streets, rocks were hurled through school windows while classes were in session, the buildings were broken into at night and robbed or wrecked. Many were burned down. Teachers were publicly whipped and even murdered if they refused to quit. In Monroe County, Mississippi, the Klan forced twenty-six teachers to close their schools. In Noxubee County three of every four schoolhouses were burned down.

Nevertheless, blacks were determined to get an education. And they managed to make impressive gains during Reconstruction. If schooling fell far short of the need, it was not the fault of the blacks. Thousands, in the face of terror, did make the leap from ignorance to knowledge.

To learn to read and write was to achieve a mental independence whites would not tolerate. Neither did whites believe blacks had any right to economic independence. The Klan was used to control and exploit black labor in many ways. Freedmen were beaten for shifting from one employer to another without permission. Whites who wanted all the jobs on the new railroads used terror to drive off black workers. On plantations, blacks whose work displeased white foremen were taken off and whipped by the Kluxers "to teach them a lesson." In some districts, when black workers fled the wholesale terror, sheriffs would arrest them on trumped-up criminal charges or on charges of violating labor contracts, and put them to forced labor. Farm laborers or sharecroppers were raided so often that many gave up sleeping at home and took to the woods every night.

During the ten years of Reconstruction, blacks held almost every kind of office in town, county and state governments. Many served in Washington. But it is a myth that Reconstruction was an era of "Negro rule." Not even in the few states where blacks were a majority did they ever "rule." Blacks did not seek racial domination, but equality. They worked willingly with whites in the Republican Party.

Only twenty-two blacks sat in Congress between 1869 and 1901. At the state level, blacks won high office and did much good in public life, but they never controlled any government. Everywhere, they had the powerful opposition of the white Democrats to contend with. And in their own Republican Party they found many whites determined to keep political power to themselves.

Clear as it became that the South was not going to become the black republic they feared, the whites never let up on their terror. It grew so great that in 1870 President Grant sent a documented report to Congress of more than 5,000 cases of Klan lynchings, floggings and other acts of violence. Congress then launched its own investigation of the Klan and published thirteen volumes of testimony on the secret society's crimes. It called the Klan "a Southern conspiracy against Constitutional law and the Negro race."

In the next few years, Congress passed three separate laws to enforce civil rights and crush the terrorists. The Ku Klux Acts, as they were called, protected voters' rights and punished persons "who shall conspire together, or go in disguise . . . for the purpose . . . of depriving any class of persons of the equal protection of the laws." The President was given power to declare martial law wherever state officials failed to keep order.

Some federal troops were sent south, and hundreds of Klansmen were arrested. There were numerous convictions, although few whites would testify against Klansmen or vote to find them guilty. And blacks knew that they risked being murdered if they dared do so. The Klan Act of 1871 ordered the Klan to disband but instead it became even more brazen, riding to commit its crimes without bothering with disguise. In 1875, Congress passed a Civil Rights Act which outlawed segregation in public places. But all these measures were crippled by court rulings and by the refusal of Southern officials to enforce the law.

Gradually the black people lost what little power they had to defend themselves. They saw most of their white allies drop out of the Republican Party. The freedmen found they were alone. In one Southern state after another the Democrats returned to power.

The support the North had once given to the freedmen faded away. A great national depression began in 1873 and Congress turned its attention to economic problems. The old radical Republican crusaders like Thaddeus Stevens and Charles Summer died, to be replaced by new Republican politicians more concerned with money and business than with racial equality and civil rights.

This was the time for the enemies of Reconstruction to come up from underground. They sensed that the North would no longer interfere. In Mississippi, for instance, the Democrats openly organized rifle clubs to overthrow the state's Reconstruction government. By riot and massacre they took control of the election of 1875 and forced the Republicans out of power.

In 1876, a Presidential election took place. The Democrats promised they would end the troubles of Reconstruction. The Republicans made it clear they were tired of fighting to keep it going. When the votes were counted, the results were very close. The ballots that would make the difference were in dispute. Each party claimed it had won. To settle the issue of who would be President, a political bargain was worked out between leaders of the two parties.

The Republicans promised to withdraw federal troops from the South. The South would be free to do as it pleased about the blacks. The Republicans also promised to give the South the economic help it wanted to rebuild the region.

In exchange for this offer, the Democrats agreed to accept

the Republican candidate as the winner of the election. So Rutherford B. Hayes took office as President in March, 1877. He promptly ordered all federal troops out of the South. The white Democrats were back in full control.

Reconstruction was over. The Klan had done its job. Terror had cleared the road to victory for white supremacy.

# 4

# "BIRTH OF A NATION" —AND REBIRTH OF THE KLAN

After the defeat of Reconstruction, the Klan was glorified as the savior of white civilization. The Klan itself faded away when its job was done. But in its brief first life it had done so much to strengthen the heritage of violence that terror persisted long after Reconstruction. Night riders appeared here and there in the South to enforce white will upon blacks and race riots exploded well into the next century.

The civil rights issue died out. Let the white South handle the "Negro problem" by itself, said the North; it knows best. What the South knew best was how to reduce the blacks to a state of peonage or semi-slavery, to ignore their rights, to deny them the right to vote by force and legal trickery.

The Supreme Court, too, beat a retreat from the civil rights front by rulings that tore away all the protections guaranteed by Constitutional amendments and federal laws. The court's decisions allowed the white South to do almost whatever it pleased with the blacks. States could exclude blacks from jury service, ban intermarriage, segregate school-children, Jim Crow public accommodations, restrict the vote to whites only, and enforce total segregation of the races.

It was a legal counter-revolution. White supremacy was once again on the throne, and protected by law. The "place" of blacks had been defined once and for all. Any talk of change was ridiculed. This view dominated public opinion. It was bolstered by scholars and scientists—historians, anthropologists, biologists, sociologists. They served the racists by preaching a theory of racial inferiority. The white race was naturally the superior, and deserved therefore to rule over the darker peoples. It was for the good of all that this should be so, it was said. To let white and black live on terms of equality would pervert scientific truth. Inevitably, mixing would destroy the racial purity of white Americans. Therefore the blacks should be segregated and, some advocated, sterilized to prevent this "lower" race from polluting the more civilized "higher" race. The same false ideas, directed against Jews instead of blacks, took hold in Europe and became the basis for Hitler's anti-Semitic program.

By 1900 *The New York Times* could write: "Northern men no longer denounce the suppression of the Negro vote in the South as it used to be denounced in Reconstruction days. The necessity of it under the supreme law of self-preservation is candidly recognized."

It seemed the Klan's program had won out. With few exceptions, the people of the whole country became convinced that full equality was impossible now, and perhaps forever. That notion justified overseas imperialism. The United States thought of itself as a white power with a mission to "civilize" the darker races in places like the Philippines.

Made politically powerless, black Americans were the victims of physical attacks. An Alabama white citizen told a black educator at Tuskegee Institute, "You understand that we have the legislature, we make the laws, we have the judges, the sheriffs, the jails, and the arms."

Violence or the threat of it was an everyday danger to black citizens. They lived in fear of attacks upon their person and their property. Beatings, mutilation, torture, lynching were so "ordinary" in the South that the newspapers hardly bothered to mention them.

Put yourself in the place of a black man or woman living in that time. (More than 90 percent of Afro-Americans lived in the South in 1910, three-fourths of them in rural areas.) From the cradle to the grave you were Jim Crowed: "White" and "Colored" signs sprouted everywhere—on stores, drinking fountains, laundries, restaurants, beaches, rooming houses, toilets, dance halls, theaters, parks, benches, funeral parlors, cemeteries, trolleys, trains. The color of your skin was the badge of inferiority. Think what it does to the human spirit to live under such open racism.

Every ounce of political and economic power was in the hands of whites set upon keeping blacks down. It was no wonder that many blacks came to feel hopeless, doomed to live for untold generations in a world of segregation and discrimination.

Not all, however. Thousands of blacks from the deep South fled to the North or West between 1890 and 1910. They wanted to break free of peonage and mob violence. Others tried to return to the ancestral homeland in Africa. Some, in the North, sought to keep alive the spark of protest that had once inflamed the abolitionists. They spoke out for racial justice and equality through several small organizations they formed. But few blacks could even hear their voices and even fewer whites listened. Without money or political strength or friendly white allies they could not influence public policy.

Even the white reformers of that period failed to protest racial injustice. They ignored the racial issue or accepted the myth that blacks were content with their lot. North or South, there was no difference in the way whites felt about blacks. Violence was just as open and vicious above the Mason Dixon Line as below it. White mobs rioted against blacks in New

York, Pennsylvania, Indiana, Ohio. In the Illinois town where Lincoln was buried—Springfield—whites savagely assaulted blacks in a two-day riot that ended with many black homes burned down, fifty blacks flogged, and two lynched. No one was punished.

The time was rotten ripe for the Ku Klux Klan to be born again. Midwife to the Klan's rebirth was a North Carolina writer named Thomas Dixon, Jr. Born in 1864, he grew up during the Reconstruction years and acquired a deep hatred for the freedmen and their white allies. He was determined "to set the record straight" on Reconstruction, and wrote a series of three novels about it. The first one, *The Leopard's Spots: A Romance of the White Man's Burden,* appeared in 1903 and was a huge success. His popularity made the public take him seriously as an authority on Reconstruction. In 1905 came the second novel, *The Clansman: An Historical Romance of the Ku Klux Klan,* and two years later, *The Traitor: A Story of the Rise and Fall of the Invisible Empire.*

The welcome given *The Clansman* caused Dixon to convert it into a play. Advertised as "The Greatest Play of the South—A Daring, Thrilling Romance of the Ku Klux Klan," it drew enormous audiences. By now a new medium, the motion picture, was becoming popular, and Dixon saw its possibilities as a means of reaching and influencing millions of people with his message of white supremacy. In 1913, he met D. W. Griffith, a pioneering film director, and interested him in producing a film version of *The Clansman.*

Griffith was a Kentuckian steeped in Southern prejudices which he never outgrew. His father had been a Confederate colonel who filled his son with sentimental, romantic tales about the Old South. Griffith was a genius who developed the new medium of the film to great artistic heights. Naturally he was excited by Dixon's story, which echoed his own racism, and the chance it offered his talents. He bought the film rights

*A still from* The Birth of a Nation *shows how Griffith's film romanticized the Klan of the Reconstruction era. The hooded riders are greeted like chivalrous knights.*

and shot the picture in Hollywood. Going far beyond the short, simple films of the time, he made the Klan story into a twelve-reel epic. It opened in New York in 1915 under the title of *The Birth of a Nation* and was a sensational success.

Dixon's novel had ignored the brutal realities of the Ku Klux Klan. The Kluxers were turned into White Knights with noble ideals who used violence only when forced to that extreme. Reconstruction was turned into a gallant fight waged by the purest of Southern whites against black monsters and their evil Yankee masters. The Klan was so glorified that old Kluxers found themselves besieged by reporters who begged for their reminiscences of those good old days. Dixon had set the example for romantic falsehood and now the veterans of the Klan embroidered upon his version of the Klan's motives and actions.

This view of the Klan was swiftly accepted by both the public and scholars. It fitted easily into the racist mentality of the time. So when the Griffith movie with its dazzling new techniques and its powerful dramatic impact was launched, its effect was to intensify the racist spirit.

Opposition to *The Birth of a Nation* was voiced at once. The editor of the New York *Post* called it "improper, immoral and unjust." The National Association for the Advancement of Colored People (born in 1910 out of revulsion against the Springfield race riot) thought the film was a travesty on historical truth and an insult to an entire race of people. Its chapters tried to prevent the showing of the film but Dixon was too much of a public relations expert for them. He turned to the President of the United States for support. Woodrow Wilson had been his classmate at college, and Dixon arranged to screen the film at the White House. After the showing, the President is said to have remarked: "It is like writing history with lightning. And my only regret is that it is all so terribly true." Dixon got the Cabinet, the Supreme Court and many

members of the Congress to see the movie, and then told the
press how much they had all liked it. Attempts to censor the
film failed. It showed to huge audiences across the country
and became one of the all-time great money-makers.

The reviews were almost all favorable. Only a very few
challenged the movie for being filled with distortions, half-
truths and downright falsifications. Rabbi Stephen Wise in
New York called it "an indescribably foul and loathsome libel
on a race of human beings." Black religious, educational and
civic groups across the nation held mass meetings to protest
and expose the film. They had small effect upon the film's
popularity.

Dixon himself admitted his motive was not to discover the
truth but to find a way to make a case for white supremacy
regardless of the facts. "The real purpose back of my film," he
wrote in May 1915 to Joseph Tumulty, President Wilson's
secretary, "was to revolutionize Northern sentiments by a
presentation of history that would transform every man in my
audience into a good Democrat! . . . Every man who comes out
of one of our theatres is a Southern partisan for life." Then,
soon after, he wrote President Wilson that the movie "is
transforming the entire population of the North and West into
sympathetic Southern voters. There will never be an issue of
your segregation policy."

A word on Woodrow Wilson: It is not surprising that
President Wilson lent the prestige of his high office to
promoting this gross distortion of history. Wilson's election in
1912, said the historian Harvard Sitkoff, "led to the most
Southern-dominated, anti-Negro national administration
since the 1850s." During his first years of office more racist bills
were introduced than in any previous Congress. His administration pushed the segregation of black government workers
and dismissed or downgraded hundreds of them. Wilson
claimed nothing could be done to improve the status of blacks

and he refused to denounce lynching publicly. His treatment of black troops in World War I was just as racist.

And what about Thomas Dixon? The historian John Hope Franklin called it a "supreme tragedy" that in *The Birth of a Nation* Dixon and Griffith succeeded in using a powerful and wonderful new instrument of communication "to perpetuate a cruel hoax on the American people that has come distressingly close to being permanent." (As we shall see later, the film has been revived again and again for over sixty-five years and used by Kluxers to help them organize.)

In the same year that *The Birth of a Nation* was being seen by millions of Americans, the Ku Klux Klan was reborn. It was the fall of 1915. Posters were put up in Atlanta to announce the opening of the movie. It gave William J. Simmons the grand moment to fulfill his dream—the revival of the KKK. Born in Alabama a few years after the end of Reconstruction, he grew up on his father's tales of his adventures while riding with the Klan. Young Simmons became a circuit preacher and spent a dozen years in the backwoods districts of the deep South. A big man, he was equally at home leading prayer, taking a snort of bourbon or making a fourth at poker. Always clean and proper, he slung a heavy gold watch chain across his ample vest and wore a diamond stickpin in his tie. When he was denied a pulpit because of "moral impairment," he turned to working for fraternal orders, selling them insurance. But why not build his own secret society and make better profits than selling the members insurance benefits? Something like the Klan his Daddy loved so much?

Perhaps the big *Birth of a Nation* posters plastering Atlanta walls with pictures of a rearing, hooded, sheet-covered horse bearing a hooded rider made him realize the moment had come to revive the glories of the Ku Klux Klan. Just before the movie opened in Atlanta, Simmons approached several men prominent in local politics and asked them to meet him

Thanksgiving at midnight atop Stone Mountain. There, under a forty-foot flaming cross, Simmons and his recruits held the ceremonies that initiated the new Klan. "We are dedicated," he proclaimed, "to maintain forever White Supremacy in all things."

That week an Atlanta newspaper published Simmons' announcement of "The World's Greatest Secret, Social, Patriotic, Fraternal, Beneficiary Order" side-by-side with the advertisement for the movie. Almost everyone who saw *Birth of a Nation* was ripe for enlistment in the Klan. The illiterate whites who could not read Dixon's novels were convinced that their own racial prejudice was justified by the movie's passionate case against black Americans.

The Klan would spread through the South and by the 1920s would become a great power in the North and West too.

# 5

## HICKS, RUBES, AND DRIVERS OF SECOND-HAND FORDS

If Simmons had not revived the Klan, someone else would probably have done it. The spirit of Kluxery was still dominant in the South. While Thomas Watson, Georgia's U.S. Senator, was not present at Stone Mountain, he was as much the father of the new Klan as Simmons.

Early in his political career Watson had tried to unite black and white farmers to work for their common needs through the Populist Party. Conservative whites wrecked his hopes by "nigger-baiting" the Populists. This split their ranks and defeated Watson's try for office. He then swung to the other side and became one of the most fiery advocates of white supremacy.

A sensational murder trial gave Watson his chance to use his brilliant oratory to climb into power. A white girl of fourteen was raped and murdered in Atlanta in 1913, and a young Jewish northerner who managed the factory she worked in was falsely charged with the crime. The Atlanta press whipped up mob hysteria against Leo Frank and he was convicted and sentenced to death. The evidence against Frank was so flimsy that a nationwide demand arose for his sentence to be commuted to life imprisonment. Watson launched an anti-Semitic crusade in his paper. When the governor of Georgia had the courage to commute Frank's sentence,

Watson turned to inciting violence. A mob of 5,000 stormed the governor's home and was stopped only by militia. Then a band of armed men broke into the state prison, kidnapped Frank, and dragged him away to be lynched from a tree.

Watson warned: "We will meet the 'Leo Frank League' with a 'Gentile League' if they provoke us much further. Another Ku Klux Klan may be organized to restore HOME RULE." And so the fiery cross atop Stone Mountain was ignited as much by Watson as by Simmons. Under William Simmons, the new Klan would follow Watson's lead and dedicate itself not only to white supremacy but to crusades against the Jews, the Catholics and immigrants.

Simmons sold memberships, Klan costumes and life insurance to his followers. "This is a white man's country," he preached to them. "The white man must be supreme, not only in America but in the world." With the country at war, Klansmen gave themselves special duties to guarantee victory and claimed that they kept a close watch on enemy aliens, slackers, union organizers and immoral women. Robed Klansmen hunted down draft-dodgers and marched in patriotic parades. By 1919, the Klan had several thousand members, their dues payments fattening Simmons' bank account.

But Simmons was not the shrewd mind the Klan needed if it was to grow to its full potential in an America boiling with

*William J. Simmons, who led the first revival of the KKK in the early twentieth century. He dedicated the new Klan to white supremacy and pledged crusades against Catholics, Jews, and immigrants.*

racial and religious prejudices. So in 1920, he made a deal with E. Y. Clarke, who ran a small publicity outfit that organized fund drives and promoted community events. Clarke saw at once the promise of big money in spreading the Klan gospel. His bargain was to take over recruiting in return for eight of every ten dollars new members would pay to join.

As soon as Clarke distributed photographs of Klansmen in full costume, the press grabbed them up. Editors were hot for any news about the KKK. Clarke knew how to create media events that would bring the Klan to public attention. He had Simmons open a Klan meeting in Georgia by silently taking a Colt automatic from his pocket and placing it on the speaker's table. Then out came a revolver from another pocket and down it went on the table, too. Now, still without a word, he took off his cartridge belt and draped it between the two guns. Then he drew out a bowie knife and stabbing it into the tabletop said solemnly: "Now let the niggers, Catholics, Jews and all others who disdain my imperial wizardry, come on!"

Clarke wrote the speeches Simmons gave, filling them with the Ten Commandments, God and Christ, purity of womanhood, morality, patriotism, the flag, and 100 percent Americanism. He trained speakers and organizers to travel around spreading the Klan's message. America was in danger, they said. Negroes, Jews, Catholics, foreigners were trying to tear down this great democracy. Only the KKK and 100 percent Americanism would save us.

The climate was right for the Klan's preachments. Americans were disillusioned by the war and its aftermath. "The good-time years," some call the 1920s. But they began with government scandals over the exploitation of public lands by oil corporations. A Senate exposure sent one Cabinet member to prison and others among President Warren Harding's cronies committed suicide or fled the country.

The next President, Calvin Coolidge, announced, "The

Business of America Is Business," and the stock market soared. Rum-runners and bootleggers flourished when Prohibition became the law, and the public turned cynical as gangsters like Al Capone achieved great wealth and power. No matter how people made their money, so long as they had a lot of it, they could move in respectable social circles. The press front-paged the sex scandals of millionaires and movie stars. Publicity could ballyhoo even swampy lots in Florida to prices incredibly above their real value.

Yes, the Twenties were good times for many Americans. The national income rose by 44 percent. Business profits shot up almost 80 percent in that same decade. It looked like the time to get rich quickly; a speculative fever took hold. Gambling on the stock market lured many and drove stock prices higher and higher.

But working people had no money to play with, and scarcely enough to live on. A 1929 economic survey showed 78 percent of the nation's families were not doing so well. They earned under $3,000 a year. And 6 million of them had incomes under $1,000 a year. Three out of four families were able to save nothing at all. The gap between incomes was wide. The 27,500 wealthiest families had as much money as the 12 million poorest families. The nation's top and bottom were worlds apart. While a miner earned $10 a week, John D. Rockefeller, Jr., paid an income tax of $6,278,000.

Many Americans were without jobs during the Twenties. Estimates range from four to nearly six million unemployed. And whole regions—the textile towns of New England, the Allegheny coal towns, the Deep South, the shipbuilding and shoe-manufacturing centers of the North—suffered hard times all through the 1920s. Farmers everywhere were in a bad way as prices for their produce slipped badly and never climbed up again.

Before the decade could get under way, twenty-five race

riots ravaged American cities. In Chicago, for 13 days the city was a battleground over which 10,000 people fought. At the end, the casualty list showed 38 killed (23 blacks and 15 whites) and 537 injured. In that one year of peace—1919—10 black veterans of World War I, still in uniform, were hung, burned, beaten or shot to death by mobs.

What the people of the small towns and countryside of America believed in crumbled under their eyes. Their religious, ethical and moral values were being trampled over at the same time that the farm economy they relied upon was collapsing. No wonder that such folk gave ready ear to a crusade against their alleged enemies. Frustrated, defeated, they could easily be diverted from grappling with their real problems to lynching "outsiders."

Behind their response, of course, was an old American intolerance of the black, the Jew, the Roman Catholic, the foreigner. The many race riots in Northern cities and the growing efforts of southerners to exclude Jews showed the way the wind was blowing. In 1922, said Simmons, the Klan's average increase in membership was 3,500 daily. Over the year it took in 1,200,000 members. Its daily income was $45,000 from members' dues and the sale of Klan regalia. At its peak in the Twenties the Klan claimed over 5 million members.

Its strength was largely in the village and rural South, and in the Midwest and West. (In none of these sections were there Jews or Catholics in any great number.) In the Midwest, the Klan's strength was in such non-urban states as Indiana, Kansas and Oklahoma.

The Klan cried for a return to the simple and virtuous life of the past. It talked racial purity. It attacked minority groups, labeling them inferior in stock and culture. It opposed the new urban life, with its mixture of many peoples, its intellectualism, its progressive politics, its changing standards of ethics and morality.

One Klan leader, Imperial Wizard Hiram Wesley Evans, described his members and their motives in a magazine article. He said the Klan was made up of "hicks and rubes and drivers of second-hand Fords." They were "plain people, very weak in the matter of culture." But they were of "the old pioneer stock, the Nordic race" responsible for "almost the whole of modern civilization." The strange ideas of liberals and leftists and minority groups about religion and politics and morality threatened them, he went on. They wanted the right to teach their children in their own schools "the fundamental facts and truths." What the Klan demanded, Evans said, was "the return of power into the hands of everyday, not highly cultured, not overly intellectualized, but entirely unspoiled and not de-Americanized, average citizens of the old stock." The Klan's aim, he concluded, was to recreate "a native, white, Protestant America."

How did it go about doing that?

# 6

## ROUGH STUFF

It takes organization to do even simple tasks well, whether in business or in politics. E. Y. Clarke's ambitions were great, and his public relations skills matched them. The Klan was politics but Clarke treated it like a business that must make a profit. He was out to sell the Klan to America and he packaged the product to appeal to the broadest groups.

First he recruited a sales force he called Kleagles. Then he divided the country into sales regions called Domains, headed by a manager called the Grand Goblin. Each region included several states, or Realms, headed by King Kleagles. Clarke himself took the title of Imperial Kleagle, while Simmons was dubbed Imperial Wizard.

To help Klan recruiters Clarke sent out experienced speakers—most of them Protestant ministers—with a sales spiel calculated to bring in the customers. America was in danger, they said, threatened by evil enemies on all sides. Whites must prepare to defend themselves against blacks, Gentiles against Jews, Protestants against Catholics, old-stock Anglo-Saxons against the new immigrants from Eastern and Southern Europe.

If those were not enemies enough to raise audiences, Clarke's advice was to hit hard on moral issues: bootlegging, dope peddling, carousing in night clubs and taverns, graft, adultery, violations of the Sabbath. Find out what your community is worried about, Clarke advised his road crews, and sell them on the Klan as the answer to their problems.

It worked. Millions paid their ten dollars to join the Invisible Empire of the Klan. They were drawn to their first meetings by Klan theater. On Saturday night, hooded horsemen would parade down Main Street, symbols of a mysterious and powerful force. Or suddenly on a Sunday morning, files of robed and masked Klansmen would silently enter the church and take seats. Then the minister—frequently a Klansman himself—would preach the Klan's gospel from the pulpit. Often the local minister would be the first in town to be approached by a Kleagle, and offered free membership and perhaps a leadership post. Many accepted, some leaving their pulpits to become full-time Klan speakers or organizers.

As each ten dollar initiation fee came in, four dollars of it went to the Kleagle recruiter, one to the state's Klan chief, 50 cents to the regional head, two-and-a-half dollars to Clarke, and two to Simmons. Because the Klan was chartered as a benevolent and charitable organization, taxes were no problem. Clarke and Simmons set up an Atlanta company to manufacture all Klan regalia, another to print its many publications, and a third to make its real estate deals.

It looked like a profitable future. But the Klan was more than preaching and profit. It meant action, too—violent action. In October 1921, the New York *World* printed an exposé of Klan violence during the previous twelve months, which was picked up by papers across the country. The KKK, it documented, was guilty of 4 killings, 1 mutilation, 1 branding with acid, 41 floggings, 27 tar-and-feather parties, five kidnappings, 43 warnings to leave town... and an unknown number of victims flattened to death under a steam roller in Louisiana.

Detailed accounts of Klan terror appeared in the press

*At a Sunday evening service in a Newark, New Jersey, church, in 1923, the minister welcomes dozens of hooded Klansmen and introduces the "Exalted Cyclops" and the "Kleagle" to his congregation. Such events were not uncommon in that decade.*

during that decade. One or two of these grim reports will serve to show what the Klan was capable of doing. In July 1921, a black man named only as "Williams" was lynched by a Klan mob in Moultrie, Georgia. Arrested on some unspecified charge, he was taken to the courthouse for a trial that lasted 30 minutes. Then sheriffs began to move him from the courtroom to the jail nearby. What followed is reported by an eyewitness in a dispatch to the Washington *Eagle*:

> Immediately a cracker by the name of Ken Murphy gave the Confederate yell: "Whoo-whoo—let's get the nigger." Simultaneously five hundred poor pecks rushed on the armed sheriffs, who made no resistance whatever. They tore the Negro's clothing off before he was placed in a waiting automobile. This was done in broad daylight. . . .
>
> The Negro was taken to a grove, where each one of more than five hundred people, in Ku Klux ceremonial, had placed a pine knot around a stump, making a pyramid to the height of ten feet. The Negro was chained to the stump and asked if he had anything to say. Castrated and in indescribable torture, the Negro asked for a cigarette, lit it and blew the smoke in the face of his tormentors.
>
> The pyre was lit and a hundred men and women, old and young, grandmothers among them, joined hands and danced around while the Negro burned. A big dance was held in a barn nearby that evening in celebration of the burning, many people coming by automobile from nearby cities to the gala event.

In 1923, a black man was lynched by the Klan for "passing as a white man." The report in the St. Louis *Argus* was brief:

EUFAULA, Okla., Nov. 7—Dallas Sewell, Negro, was
seized by a group of men wearing garb of the Ku Klux
Klan and, after a Klan trial in the barn of a well-
known Klansman, was hanged this morning to a barn
rafter.

Sewell was found guilty of "passing for white and
associating with white women" and he was therefore
put to death in accordance with the Klan "Kode."

The lynching of blacks in the South pyramided rapidly after
the era of Reconstruction. It was done to terrorize them and to
maintain white supremacy. From 1882 to 1927, as many as
3,405 blacks were lynched in seventeen Southern and border
states. A folk tradition holds that lynchers killed their victims
only for the crimes of rape or murder. (As though *any* crime
could justify such illegal mob action.) But statistics demonstrate that many were murdered for alleged minor offenses or
simply out of racial prejudice.

The lynchings were appallingly sadistic. Burning, mutilation
and torture of the helpless victims were common. How many
such recorded crimes can be laid to the Klan, it is impossible to
determine. In many cases robed Klansmen publicly took part
and the Klan sought credit for the lynching. In all cases a Klan
mentality certainly animated the lynchers. Not only men but
women and children were often participants or eager observers.

One obvious reason that the Klan's role in violence cannot
always be documented is the fear inspired in the victims. When
Klansmen flogged someone, they ordered him to be silent
about it—or even to leave the district—on pain of suffering
even worse. Hundreds of Alabamans—black and white—had
been kidnapped and lashed by the Klan in the years 1922–27,
said the Birmingham *News*. Their crime? Mostly selling liquor
or owning slot machines. If some victims were brave enough to

report the violence, usually nothing was done about it. It was the same as in Reconstruction days: local officials were themselves part of the Klan machinery. So the Klan operated behind walls of silence.

The Klan had appointed itself the defender of purity and virtue, embodied in 100 percent Americanism. That meant taking action against their enemies, the "sinners" and "devils." Action for the Klan was not words but violence. Its members, sworn to secrecy and to protection of their fellow Klansmen, felt safe in unleashing violent impulses through group terror. Alone, they might have feared to do what they could do when joined by other wearers of the robe.

Klan leaders were always threatening "rough stuff" and many Klan units had special strong-arm squads who wore black robes and special insignia. "There are lots of fellows who want just a little of the rough stuff," E. Y. Clarke told a meeting in Tulsa. "If you crave any of this rough stuff be sure that you get qualified to go up into the third degree."

Even if the national leaders had wanted to prevent crimes, they could not have stopped local Klans from doing as they pleased. One historian of the Klan, David M. Chalmers, estimates there were over a thousand victims of Klan assaults during the Twenties just in Texas and Oklahoma. He puts down over a hundred cases each in Florida, Georgia, and Alabama, dozens in California, and scattered numbers in the Midwest and Mountain states. Riots and open warfare marked Klan life in Indiana, Ohio, and Pennsylvania.

During a Pennsylvania courtroom fight in 1927 over control of the Klan, witnesses took the stand to describe Klan secrets and horrors. They told of a small girl kidnapped from her grandparents in Pittsburgh, of a Colorado Klansman beaten to death when he tried to resign, of a man in Terrell, Texas, soaked in oil and burned to death before a mob of hundreds of Kluxers. One unexpected side of such reports was how often it was not blacks, Jews or Catholics who felt the Klan's terror, but white Anglo-Saxon Protestants.

Nevertheless, Jews and Catholics were among the main targets of Klan attack. The Klan was set up for native-born white Protestants, which meant the Jew was an outsider, and therefore an enemy. When hard times hit, Jewish bankers were blamed. If someone's business was doing badly, it was the fault of Jewish competitors. If citizens were fearful of the threat of war, then international Jewry was stirring up trouble. If strikes broke out, Jewish radicals were accused of agitating the workers.

Catholics—there were far more of them than Jews—were considered a prime menace by the Klan. It even published a fake "Knights of Columbus Oath" in which Catholics were pledged to "hang, burn, boil, flay and bury alive" all non-Catholics. The forged document was as vicious and as widely distributed as the "Protocols of the Elders of Zion," which alleged a Jewish plot to rule the world. The only good Catholics were dead Catholics, said Klan leaders. Catholics could never be assimilated into American life the Klan warned, because the Pope controlled them from Rome.

In the Klan's view, none of the newcomers from Eastern and Southern Europe belonged here. America's immigration policy had long been an open door for all who wished to enter. What else was America but a nation of nations? Still, there were always some who feared "foreigners." From the early 1800s, the Irish immigrants had been pictured as agents of the Pope sent to subvert America. In the 1850s the Know-Nothings, a political party of "native" Americans, had sprung up to keep foreigners and especially Catholics from public office, and to make immigration more difficult.

The Chinese were the next target. In 1882 Congress

slammed the door shut against them. Just at that time a new mass wave of immigration from Eastern and Southern Europe began. Again the nativists tried to keep them out. Prejudice against the latecomers soon became a habit. When immigrants began coming in again after World War I, the nativists called for a quota system, and laws passed in 1921 kept out almost all the people of Eastern and Southern Europe while giving preference to the old Nordic groups. The Klan joined other nativists to press for still another restrictive measure which Congress adopted in 1924. Again and again the Klan proved how rigidly racist it was. Anyone not of Nordic stock was inferior, and unfit to become a true American.

# 7

# POLITICS AND POWER

By 1925 the Klan was Big Business. Almost six million Americans belonged to it during the Twenties, and they paid $75 million a year into its treasury. That August, caravans of cars and dozens of chartered trains bearing Kluxers from around the nation poured into the city of Washington with KKK signs chalked on their sides. On Saturday afternoon, August 8, forty thousand hooded Klansmen and women paraded down Pennsylvania Avenue to the Washington Monument. Their marching bands blared "Onward Christian Soldiers" and as the crowds lining the sidewalks cheered, the Kluxers raised their right arms in salute.

The peak of Klan power came during the 1920s. So strong had the Klan become that in Oregon it was able to elect the President of the State Senate and the Speaker of the House. In Ohio, where perhaps 400,000 joined the Invisible Empire, Klan-supported candidates became mayors of Toledo, Akron, Columbus. In Texas, 200,000 joined, and Earl Mayfield was the first Klansman to be elected to the U.S. Senate. In Waco the Mayor and Board of Police Commissioners were Klansmen. So were scores and scores of sheriffs throughout the state. In California the Klan captured the state legislature with its candidates.

*In the nation's capital, 40,000 hooded Klansmen and women parade down Pennsylvania Avenue on Saturday afternoon, August 18, 1925. This event marked the peak of the Klan's power in the Twenties.*

In an Arkansas election the Klan swept almost every office in Little Rock. The Klan was so entrenched in Alabama that it could elect Klansmen Bibb Graves and Charles McCall governor and attorney general. Klan candidates were elected mayor of Emporia and to other local offices in Kansas.

William Allen White, editor of the Emporia *Gazette,* urged all citizens to oppose the Klan:

> The Ku Klux Klan is an organization of cowards. Not a man in it has the courage of his convictions. It is an organization of traitors to American institutions. Not a man in it has faith enough in American courts, laws and officials, to trust them to maintain law and order. . . . It is a menace to peace and decent neighborly living. . . . For a self-constituted body of moral idiots who would substitute the findings of the Ku Klux Klan for the processes of law, to try to better conditions, would be a most un-American outrage which every good citizen should resent.
>
> It is a national menace, this Klan. It knows no party. It knows no country. It knows only bigotry, malice and terror. Our national government is founded upon reason, and the Golden Rule. This Klan is preaching terror and force.

The Klan won so many followers in Indiana that in 1923 it could assemble 100,000 of them in a field near Kokomo to crown David Stephenson the Grand Dragon of the Realm of Indiana. "He sold fright," said a reporter, "as he had sold coal, in carload lots." He paraded legions of his hooded knights through black and Catholic districts of the cities. Enrolling 240,000 members in the state, he elected two senators, two governors and the legislature. For a while he made the state an appendage to the Klan.

New York put 200,000 Klansmen on the rolls and Pennsylvania 225,000. In the New England states, Connecticut provided 20,000 and Maine 15,000.

Except for Indiana, the Klan did best in the state of Colorado. It began its work in Denver in 1921 and in scarcely three years converted the state into one of its strongest realms. Enlisting 35,000 members, the Klan became the dominant power in state and local politics. Under Grand Dragon John G. Locke, it took over the Republican Party and in the 1924 election won control of Colorado. The Klan elected a U.S. Senator, the governor, lieutenant-governor, secretary of state, attorney general, superintendent of public instruction, and a state supreme court justice. Skillful political organizing methods at the grass roots level did it. Once in office, the Klan governor filled every position he could with Klansmen.

The presidential election of 1924 gave the Klan a chance to show its national strength. At the Democratic Convention in New York it is estimated that at least 350 delegates—over one-fourth of the total number—were Klansmen. They were responsible for defeating an anti-Klan plank in the platform and for the failure of Governor Alfred Smith, a Catholic, to win the party's nomination.

The Republicans offered little better. Their candidate, President Calvin Coolidge, believed the White House should do nothing about lynching, disfranchisement, or discrimination in federal employment. When some delegates proposed an anti-Klan plank at the Republican Convention, the leadership had it quietly buried in committee.

The next presidential contest, in 1928, stood out because of a carefully orchestrated whispering campaign that played on religious prejudice. This time Alfred Smith had won the Democratic nomination. The Republicans spread it about that if he entered the White House the Pope would come to Washington to run the country. The Klan preferred the

Republican candidate, Herbert Hoover. Although he was a Quaker, that was some sort of Protestant. Again the Klan scattered nationwide copies of its phony "Knights of Columbus Oath." Scary headlines in its press read: ROMAN CATHOLIC CLERICAL PARTY OPENS BIG DRIVE TO CAPTURE AMERICA FOR THE POPE. Smith's supporters confronted the issue, called the election a battle between Smith and the Klan. But 1928 was not a Democratic year, and Hoover won.

What the election showed was that America was not immune to intolerance. The appeal to racial and religious prejudice that Hitler was making in Germany in those years found response among millions here, too.

Taking power proved easier for the Klan than using it. Colorado's Klan administration failed to produce results to please anyone and, after one term in office, was defeated. Nationwide, the Klan crumbled and disintegrated by the end of the Twenties. When Klansmen gained office, hostile legislators and bureaucrats often managed to block them. As the movement lost its political influence, its followers dropped away.

Scandals, too, did much to bleed the Klan. As early as 1921 a Congressional investigation exposed Klan racketeering. Even while the Klan rode high in Colorado, for instance, its violence and corruption came to light and decline set in. David Stephenson, Indiana's Klan leader, was convicted of raping and murdering a young woman and sent to prison for life.

National and state Klan leaders struggled for control, and in their attempts to unseat one another, exposed how they abused the powers of their offices and violated the Klan's proclaimed principles of moral decency. Internal quarrels disheartened the membership and weakened the Klan's reputation and power. When driven out of office, some leaders formed Klan-like rival organizations and then became ensnared in costly lawsuits that did the Klan still more damage. Many Klan groups gave up and disbanded. Members who thought they had joined to fight for morality found too much immorality within their own ranks. The Klan's pure white robes had become stained and dishonored.

Why did the Klan fail after reaching so much power? Sociologists studying the life of such movements have offered some answers. They think that the Klan of the Twenties never had inspiring leaders or any great unifying ideals. It was planless and opportunistic. Its program was defensive. It preached action against evils which were often more imaginary than real. Like its ancestor of Reconstruction days, it was loosely organized with no central commanding authority. Like that first Klan, it was also anti-democratic, violent, uncontrollable. Historian David Chalmers concludes: "The failure of the Ku Klux Klan to anchor itself as a successful feature in American life was due more to its own ineptness than any other cause or combination of factors. The decline of the Klan as a mass movement in America was its own fault, nobody else's."

Which leads one to ask: suppose its terror had not gone so far, its leaders had not been so inept, its program not so negative? What would have happened to America?

# 8

# DEPRESSION AND WAR

It was the stock market crash of October 1929 that signaled the slide into the pit. At first it seemed to be only another depression. America had already gone through many of them. Could another one be any worse? But the crisis which began that year was different. It came on harder and faster, it engulfed a much larger part of the population, it lasted much longer, and it did far more damage than any before it.

By 1932 one out of every four workers was jobless. Almost half the country's industry was idle. Family savings shrank to nothing, credit was used up, mortgages were foreclosed, children and adults went to bed hungry. People got sick and couldn't afford medical care. By the spring of 1933 the country was the nearest it had ever been to complete collapse.

At first most people believed that hard times were a matter of bad luck and joblessness was their own fault. But as time passed and the blight spread, workers and farmers and middle class people saw that they were the ones who suffered most. For the rich, life only became a bit more complicated. Rockefellers and Vanderbilts didn't starve, nor were they evicted from their homes because they couldn't pay their rent.

The millions of sufferers began to look for political cures for their troubles. A number of social movements sprang up, making appeals of many kinds for followers. They ran all the way from the far right politically to the far left. There was the German American Bund, which echoed Hitler's Nazi program. There was Father Coughlin's National Union of Social Justice, which blamed the Jews for America's crisis. There was Huey Long's populist Share the Wealth movement, and Upton Sinclair's utopian socialist EPIC campaign. There were the Socialist and the Communist parties that had been around long before but saw in the Great Depression a chance to build a mass movement.

The Klan was in poor shape when the depression came on. Its ranks had thinned so badly in the late 1920s that the organization was reduced almost to a skeleton. With hard times, many of the remaining members could no longer pay their dues. They were more concerned with survival than with mummery. If any Klan leader had been able to offer a solution to the economic crisis, he might have rallied a new following. Instead, the Klan could only offer this feeble prescription for the New Year:

> *And here's hoping*
> *That you keep*
> *Smiling Thru*
> *1931—with Ku Klux Klan*

Unable to propose positive programs, the Klan pushed only two defensive measures: First, keep foreigners out and kick out those already here. (That would make more jobs.) The second idea was to be patriotic. That meant don't do anything "un-American," like demonstrating for jobs or unemployment relief. In Ohio, the Klan's Grand Dragon said that the hungry people who demonstrated in the state capital were nothing but "Negroes, Hunks, Dagoes and the rest of the scum of Europe's slums."

After Franklin D. Roosevelt became President in March 1933, the Klan attacked him for bringing "too many Jews and Catholics" into government. The New Deal, it charged, had "honeycombed Washington with Communists." By 1936 the Klan was calling Communism the main enemy.

During the depression decade Florida's Klan became the biggest realm in the country. It added new chapters and built its ranks to about 30,000 members. Again it trumpeted, "This is a white man's country," as it tried to intimidate blacks and prevent them from voting. The Klan went after "immoral" behavior, raiding night clubs, strip joints, gambling parlors, houses of prostitution. Any kind of behavior the Klan disapproved of—from labor organizing to nude bathing—was called "communistic." And again night riders appeared to flog and terrorize the Klan's victims.

In Florida's citrus country the growers feared union organization because it would reduce profits. The Klan became a ready weapon to use against the trade unions. The new CIO, which birthed powerful mass unions in the Thirties, was called by the Klan a "subversive, radical, Red organization." Organizers who tried to recruit field workers in the citrus groves disappeared into the night never to be seen again. The Klan boasted it took good care of such "troublemakers."

In Tampa an independent political party, the Modern Democrats, campaigned to rid the city of its corrupt political machine. The movement was led by Joseph Shoemaker, an organizer of a union of relief workers and the unemployed. One night late in November 1935, masked men kidnapped Shoemaker and drove him to an isolated spot where they flogged and castrated him, then plunged his leg into a bucket of boiling tar. Nine days later he died in agony. The horror roused national protest, perhaps because this time the lynching victim was not black, but white. Committees of unionists, civil liberties advocates and others were formed to seek justice. Eleven men were indicted for the crime, most of them city employees and members of the Klan. Despite the damaging evidence, all the defendants went free.

In North Carolina a union tried to organize textile

workers. It built a biracial unemployment council in Green-ville, which led the jobless in demands for ten-dollars-a-week work relief, free house rent, and the abolition of chain gangs. The city was a Klan stronghold, and when jobless workers came to testify before the town council, robed and masked Kluxers stood menacingly in the hall. Two nights later a hundred masked Klansmen raided a meeting of the unem-ployed and beat up blacks and whites. The police did nothing, leaving it to the Klan to drive out this "communist" organiza-tion.

In South Carolina the Klan posted hundreds of placards around the textile mills, warning workers to stay away from the union. The Klan patrolled union meeting halls and planted fiery crosses in front of the homes of union-minded workers. In Atlanta the Klan flogged the textile organizer and the workers who signed up with him. It helped elect E. D. Rivers, the Georgia governor, once a paid lecturer for the Klan, and in return he put Imperial Wizard Hiram Evans on his staff. (Later Evans, who had succeeded Simmons, was indicted for using his public office for private profit.)

In was in the Midwest that some ex-Klansmen started a new Klan-like organization called the Black Legion. It began in Detroit as a club of migrants from the hill country of the South; they had come north in search of factory jobs. When two members were fired from their jobs, their former boss was taken to a Black Legion meeting and ordered to rehire the men or be executed. The threat worked, and new members flocked into Legion lodges that sprang up in the industrial centers of Michigan, Indiana, and Ohio—all states where the Klan had been a power in the Twenties. The recruits were mostly factory workers, public employees and petty politicians.

The Legion imitated the Klan's ritual and secrecy. It turned from white to black robes and hoods, but relied on the same weapons of terror—the lash, the gun, the bomb. And like the Klan, it soon began to thirst for political power. It elected hundreds of public officials in the Midwest, appealing to anti-Catholic, anti-black and anti-Semitic prejudice.

Workers organizing the auto plants were hounded relent-lessly by the Legion. Dozens of organizers were kidnapped, beaten and tortured. At least ten whom the Legion condemned to death as communists were killed. Governor George H. Earle of Pennsylvania publicly charged that such big business leaders as those at DuPont and General Motors were financing the Legion in the hope of smashing the growing labor movement. The LaFollette Senate Committee, investigating anti-labor practices, charged in 1939 that the National Association of Manufacturers saw "Communism behind every move designed to improve the lot of labor." The Committee added that the employer "cloaks his hostility to labor" under "the pretext that he is defending himself and the country against Communism."

The Klan was so busy with its attacks upon the labor movement that it told its Kleagles to forget about the Jews, the Catholics, and the blacks, and to concentrate on the CIO. Imperial Wizard Evans shrilled that the CIO "was infested with communists, led by aliens," and was out to plunge the country into "industrial war."

Dozens of small groups came into being in the Thirties, preaching the same hates cherished by the Klan. They ran the color gamut in costume and name—the Silver Shirts, the Khaki Shirts, the Blue Shirts, the White Band. Other such groups paraded in religious guise—the Christian Mobilization and the Christian Front. Like the brown-shirted Nazi storm troopers in Germany, they drilled their followers in religious prejudice and race hatred. Wherever men and women rebelled against inequality and injustice and insisted upon their rights, these vigilante groups tried to terrorize them.

Investigative reporters of that time discovered many links between the Klan and these native fascist groups. Most damning were the joint mass meetings staged by the Klan and the German-American Bund, decorated by fiery crosses and fiery swastikas. At one of these a Bund leader, August Klapprott, proclaimed that "the principles of the Bund and the principles of the Klan are the same."

Several Bund leaders were indicted for sedition when the war against Hitler began. The Institute for Propaganda Analysis warned that such fascist groups were brewing a poison mixed of equal parts of anti-union, anti-leftist, anti-Semitic and anti-black bigotry. The Southern writer W. J. Cash called Nazi ideas on race "Ku Kluckery." And the editor of the Atlanta *Constitution*, Ralph McGill, wrote: "We can't do much pointing of the accusing finger at Adolf Hitler or ell Doochey [Mussolini] for trying to give their people an exaggerated idea of the supremacy of their blood. We have the Klan."

The entry of America into World War II put the Klan in the unhappy position of supporting enemy propaganda. When some thirty Americans were indicted for sedition, it turned out that the Klan had been dealing with a good many of them. So the Klan tried an about-face. It denounced the Axis powers, promoted war bonds and called for unity of all factions to win the war. It even suspended publication of its reprint of *The International Jew*, the vicious anti-Semitic tract originally published by Henry Ford, which the Nazis had distributed in Germany, too.

But the Klan never let up on its attacks against minorities and the unions. In June 1943, 25,000 workers at the Packard plant in Detroit—which made engines for bombers and boats—struck in protest against the upgrading of three blacks. It was a wildcat strike strongly opposed by the union leadership. The union charged that the fomenters of the strike were members of the KKK. Kluxers in the plant had bitterly opposed the hiring and promotion of black workers despite the desperate shortage of labor. The Packard managers had openly urged the strikers to hold out in their demand for getting rid of black workers. Within a few hours the city was a battlefield. The mayor and the police did nothing to stop the mob. It took federal troops to establish a curfew and halt the rioting. The thirty hours of street battle cost Detroit 34 lives, injuries to over 600 people, the destruction of millions of dollars worth of property, and the halting of war production during the rioting. Of the 34 dead, 25 were blacks, 17 of them killed by the police. More than three-fourths of the injured were black. And 85 percent of the 1,800 arrested were blacks who had been attacked, not the attackers.

In 1944, the Klan closed its imperial offices in Atlanta and suspended the charters of the local chapters. This was only a dodge to avoid trouble with the law. It meant the local Klaverns could do as they pleased, relieving the top leadership of all responsibility. Many of the Klaverns tried to avoid legal trouble by taking on a variety of new names while the war lasted.

One Klansmen who did not bother to hide his identity was J. B. Stoner, the Kleagle of Tennessee. He announced that Hitler was "too easy" on the Jews, not getting rid of enough of them. "Anti-Semitism and white supremacy go hand in hand," he said. As the war neared its end, Klan action picked up again. In Georgia, Virginia, New Jersey, Texas, signs of its revival appeared. Along the highway leading into Miami the Klan erected two billboards reading, "The Ku Klux Klan Welcomes You," giving a post office box number.

In the fall of 1946, the Klan burned its first cross since Pearl Harbor, atop Stone Mountain. Atlanta again became the organizing center for the KKK. One of its first campaigns sought to kill the extension of the wartime Fair Employment Practices Committee. From California to New York, Klan chapters showed fresh signs of life. It was the old Klan, but now out to recruit returned GIs struggling to find a place in civilian life. Jews, blacks, Catholics, labor organizers again were labeled the enemy.

But this time the Klan met strong opposition. The U.S. Attorney General, Tom Clark of Texas, said he would use every law on the book to break up the Klan. He instructed the Justice Department to search for Klan violations of federal law and interference with civil rights. No court actions were brought, but the fear of them may have slowed up some Kluxers. When the Attorney General issued a list of subversive organizations in 1947, the Klan was placed alongside the Communist Party, one of its pet enemies. Far more was done, however, to ferret out radicals than to hinder the Klan.

Some of the states did more than Washington to get after the Klan. California, Pennsylvania, New York, New Jersey, Michigan, Ohio, Indiana, Kentucky—all took measures of varying kinds to banish the Klan or to curtail its activities. Georgia's liberal governor, Ellis Arnall, set out to revoke the Klan's charter on the ground that it was anything but the nonprofit, charitable, benevolent society it was supposed to be. Under pressure, the Klan gave up its national charter but continued to operate within Georgia. Its chief effort was to keep blacks from the polls by intimidation and terror.

In many states and cities new laws and ordinances were designed to hamper the Klan by making public use of the mask grounds for conviction. Fines and jail sentences were laid on for masked misdeeds. Still, in the early 1950s bombs were set off at a Florida Jewish school and synagogue. Sticks of dynamite were planted beside a Catholic church. A dynamite blast killed the state's NAACP leader, Harry Moore, and his wife. Klan floggings continued to occur in the South, with occasional arrests and sometimes a conviction. But in these postwar years the Klan never reached the impressive power it had attained in the 1920s. Was the country no longer willing to listen to the Klan's message?

# 9

# YOU THINK YOU GOT A RIGHT TO VOTE?

It is the night of September 2, 1957, when Edward Aaron runs into the Ku Klux Klan by chance. Aaron, thirty-four, is a quiet, slim black man, living with his mother on the edge of Birmingham, Alabama. He has served honorably with the Army in England and the Philippines and now is a painter's helper. On this unlucky evening he is walking along a country road with a woman friend when six men in cars drive up. Members of a local KKK chapter, they are out to see if one of their group, Bart Floyd, can qualify for leadership. The test? To prove himself by showing he is willing "to get nigger blood on his hands."

This is what happens next:

The cars stopped, and before the Negroes could suspect danger the Klansmen leaped on Aaron and threw him into the back of Floyd's car. Aaron said: "Whatya want with me? I ain't done nothin'!" Floyd answered by slugging him with a pistol, then sitting on him while Mabry drove Floyd's car about six miles to the lair.

At the lair the Klansmen unlocked the door and lighted the lamps. Then they brought in "the nigger." None of them knew him or had ever seen him. They addressed him only as *nigger* or *you black sonofabitch*. Not once did they allow him to stand erect. They made him crawl out of the car, then crawl to the entrance of the lair and inside. They made him sit on his knees and watch them put on their robes and hoods. Pritchett, as Cyclops, put on a red hood adorned with gold. The hood looked like a pillowcase; it had slits for the eyes but no slits for the ears or mouth. Pritchett's robe and the robes and hoods of the others were white.

Aaron, kneeling in the dirt and lamplight, knew he was helpless. He didn't even have a pocket knife. There were no houses nearby; he could scream his head off and no one would hear. . . .

For half an hour the group baited their helpless victim. With curses, kicks, and four-letter filth they "interrogated the nigger." They knew three "hate" names—Chief Justice Earl Warren; Martin Luther King, who a year earlier had led the Montgomery bus boycott; and a local Negro preacher who was then leading an effort to integrate the railroad station. They used these names in the "interrogation."

"Look at me, nigger! You think you're as good as I am! You think any nigger is as good as a white man!"

"Look here, nigger! You ever heard of a nigger-loving Communist named Earl Warren? You ain't? Well, you ought to learn who he is, because he loves you!"

"Look at me, nigger! You got any kids? You think nigger kids should go to school with my white kids? You think you got a right to vote? Or eat where I eat? Or use the same toilet I use?"

Finally the Kluxers end the baiting with action. They slug Aaron with a pistol, dazing him. Then they tear off his clothes, spreadeagle him in the dirt, and watch while Floyd castrates him with a razor.

Aaron is tossed into a car trunk, driven off some miles, and thrown out on the side of the road.

Bart Floyd has proved himself worthy to lead the Klan.

And Edward Aaron, the Klan thinks, has been taught how to be a "good nigger."

To be good? That meant to be quiet. A "good" Southern town was a peaceful town, peaceful because no blacks challenged the system of segregation and discrimination. That peace was never universal and always only on the surface. And now it had been broken. Step by step through the 1930s and 1940s the NAACP had carried the fight for the franchise and for equal educational opportunities through the courts.

On May 17, 1954, came the sweeping decision of the U.S. Supreme Court—with Earl Warren as Chief Justice—that persons "required on the basis of race to attend separate schools were deprived of the equal protection of the law guaranteed by the Fourteenth Amendment." Racial segregation in the public schools was outlawed. The "separate but equal" doctrine the Court had upheld in 1896 was set aside.

Millions of blacks rejoiced that at last—almost ninety years after Emancipation—the basic rights of democracy for all were recognized.

But soon resistance to the Court's ruling developed. The battle for school desegregation became international news. Clinton, Nashville, Atlanta, Little Rock, Oxford—the names flashed across the world's front pages. Refusal to comply with the law ranged from simple inaction through token integration to riots and bombings.

Only a few months after the court ruling, the White Citizens Council was born in Mississippi. The middle class organization multiplied rapidly throughout the South. It said its aim was to preserve segregation by legal means. But many councils went far beyond the bounds of the law. They turned to open and hidden terror, to economic pressure, to reprisals against whites who stood up for the law. "We intend to make it difficult, if not impossible," said a Council leader, "for any Negro who advocates desegregation to find and hold a job, get credit, or renew a mortgage."

The Klan had shrunk to a handful of chapters by the early

1950s. Now it was reborn. Klaverns sprang up all over the South like thistles after rain. They swore allegiance to any one of many self-annointed Wizards who declared that "his Klan and his alone was the sole surviving splinter of the true Klan cross."

Kluxers of the late Fifties went in for more than tough talk. They leaped up on the stage of the Birmingham Audi-torium to attack singer Nat "King" Cole during a concert, and they organized a riot on the campus of the University of Alabama to force the trustees to expel the first black student they had admitted. They turned Clinton, Tennessee, into a raging mob town when the schools were integrated. They bombed black and white schools in many cities. In Nashville they blew a leader of the NAACP out of bed with a bomb. At the University of Mississippi they shot a newspaperman dead when James Meredith enrolled there as a student.

The toll of terrorism was staggering. In 1959 *The New York Times* reported "530 specific cases of violence, reprisal and intimidation" over the preceding four-year period in Atlanta alone. It said that resistance groups such as the KKK had spread across the South. "Gunpowder and dynamite, parades and cross burnings, anonymous telephone calls, beatings and threats have been the marks of their trade." When Mack Parker was lynched in 1959 the New York *Age* noted he was "the 578th human being in Mississippi who has met death at the hands of a mob since 1882."

Commonplace as the Klan's violence was in this period, its membership did not climb high. One reason was the miserable leadership. Many of the Wizards and Dragons used the Klan chiefly as a means to make a dollar. Many others had criminal records. Some were psychopaths. Others were too stupid to do anything well. "Although they dreamed big," as one historian wrote, "they thought small."

The real leaders of the South tried to be more subtle in

their opposition to desegregation. They preferred economic and political pressure to violence. The business community likes law and order; violence is bad for business.

But the Klan and the other vigilante groups got mixed signals from the middle and upper classes. Much of the establishment was for white supremacy, too. Political and civil leaders pledged resistance and practiced it as well, if not by violent means. So while they seemed to disapprove of Klan terror, they really did little to stop it.

Victims of the Klan could not expect more. As Ralph McGill, publisher of the Atlanta *Constitution*, put it: "In a small community you too often find that the sheriff is a member or that the deputies are members. And the poor white man, or more particularly the poor Negro, well knows that he has no protection at all. The law isn't going to help him because the law is, more often than not, in the Klan or sympathetic with it. . . ."

Even where the authorities attempted to halt terror, the Klan's cross burnings and floggings went on. Southern police once set up a special intelligence operation, but they nailed few bombers. And those they caught were usually acquitted.

By the opening of the 1960s the Klan showed a renewed interest in anti-Semitism. It distributed the literature of professional anti-Semites and wove its themes into the Klan's standard appeals. School integration became "a Communist-Jewish conspiracy plotting to overthrow white-Christian mankind." Synagogues and temples were bombed, with the Jews accused of doing it themselves to win sympathy. The Holocaust didn't happen, the anti-Semites claimed, while regretting that Hitler hadn't killed all the Jews. When a Kluxer was arrested he called himself a victim of Jewish persecution. Klans began using the Nazi salute, and some dressed in storm trooper outfits and displayed the swastika symbol.

To meet the violent direct action of the Klan and other

terrorist groups, a new technique was created. Blacks decided
to take matters into their own hands. Nonviolent direct action,
a form of mass resistance, emerged as the means of advancing
the struggle for civil rights. Montgomery, Alabama, the cradle
of the Confederacy, was its birthplace the day courageous Mrs.
Rosa Parks refused to move to the Jim Crow section of the bus.
That act of defiance began the great Montgomery bus boycott
of 1955–56, led by the Rev. Martin Luther King, Jr. The
Montgomery blacks won their battle, and the boycott was
picked up throughout the country as the weapon that could
force change.

What we were telling the white community, said Rev.
King, was "we can no longer lend our cooperation to an evil
system." The victory of the bus boycott was a turning point.
New times had come. New leaders came out of that long trial,
young men and women native to the South, helped by but not
dependent upon Northern friends. As the U.S. Supreme Court
went on with ban after ban against Jim Crow, blacks were
affirmed in their deep feelings that they were right in their
protest, that direct action could produce the social change
justice demanded.

Violent opposition to the new black revolution for civil
rights did not cease. Three times Martin Luther King's home
was shot up or bombed—and finally he was assassinated. But
the struggle went on. Another chapter opened early in 1960
when black college students in Greensboro, North Carolina, sat
down at a lunch counter in Woolworth's and vowed that they
and others would stay there until blacks were served. The sit-in
won national attention, and the protest method soon brought
desegregation to theaters, amusement parks, libraries, beaches,
swimming pools, churches, hotels, buses, trains, and terminals.

The tactics of the white supremacists changed. Instead of
arresting demonstrators for violating segregation ordinances,
local officials flung them into jail for disorderly conduct or

creating disturbances. The cases had to go to court, taking years on appeal and costing heavily for bonds.

But direct action continued. It won victories in some places, failed in others. Yet it succeeded in applying the vast pressure needed to obtain passage of a new federal Civil Rights Act which put the immediate goals of the movement into law.

One of the provisions of that law allowed the Justice Department to challenge voting discrimination. Back in 1870 the Fifteenth Amendment had guaranteed that "The right of citizens of the United States shall not be denied or abridged by the United States or by any State on account of race, color, or previous condition of servitude." Simple words. But they had not been respected in the South for nearly one hundred years. When Reconstruction was overthrown, the right to vote was gradually cut down until it was now only a paper promise.

In Mississippi, for instance, very few blacks were allowed to vote. In 1964 only 5 percent of the blacks in that state were registered. White supremacy had ruled for generations and it did not mean to give up its power. Even after the new Civil Rights Act of 1957, little progress was made. Some said it was because Washington was not really trying. Southern officials made their own law, without regard for the Constitution, and the federal government acted as though it had no power to do anything about it.

Then in 1960, Mississippi began to move toward a new day. The Student Nonviolent Coordinating Committee (SNCC) started a campaign to register blacks to vote. It opened voter registration schools in county after county, soon aided by the Congress of Racial Equality, the Southern Christian Leadership Conference, and the NAACP.

The new Voter Education Project reached thousands of blacks in Mississippi in the next few years. It expanded to a special civil rights program which aimed at massive education and community improvement as well as voter registration.

White Mississippi answered peaceful progress with savage violence. When students marched in Jackson they were met with clubs, tear gas and police dogs. In Biloxi, blacks trying to swim at a public beach were attacked with clubs and chains by a white mob and ten were wounded by gunfire. Alabama was the Klan's stronghold in those early Sixties. Eugene "Bull" Connor, Birmingham's police commissioner, was as ready to use violent tactics as the Klan. It was hard to tell whether Klansmen or police were to blame for bombings. The state-house, ruled by Governors John Patterson and then George Wallace, never showed distaste for violence against "nigger lovers."

In the rest of the South the terror was often as fanatical. But black Americans refused to retreat. The stereotype of the faithful, hard-working black maid or handyman was smashed on millions of TV screens. The student movement jolted the older defense organizations into a new dynamism, and civil disobedience became the technique to bring about social change on a national scale.

In some places the Klan tried to imitate the civil rights activists. When blacks picketed a store or restaurant, the Klan countered with its own picket lines and leaflets. It called rallies and took part in political campaigns. Alabama's Imperial Wizard, Robert Shelton, began to urge fresh tactics. "Let's be

*As desegregation of public facilities spread in the 1960s, the Klan took to the streets in a vain attempt to halt the movement. Here the KKK pickets a newly desegregated hotel in Atlanta, Georgia.*

nonviolent," he said in 1963. "We've got to start fighting just like the niggers." He proposed Klan marches, registration drives, boycotts and sit-ins.

How little that meant! That year a bomb exploded in a Baptist Church in Birmingham, killing four little black girls and injuring scores of others attending Sunday school. The same year NAACP Field Secretary Medgar Evers was gunned down in the doorway of his home in Jackson, Mississippi. In 1965 a protest march from Selma to Montgomery, Alabama, was attacked by deputy sheriffs and state troopers using cattle prods, whips, tear gas and clubs. Many of the marchers were badly hurt. One white marcher, Mrs. Viola Liuzzo, mother of five children, was murdered when Kluxers shot into her car as she was driving on the highway.

Soon after, Georgia Klansmen fired a shotgun blast into the car of a black educator, Lemuel Penn, and killed him. "When such an order as this [the Klan] moves in and takes over the police power," said Attorney General Richmond Flowers of Alabama, "you are completely at their mercy, and their atrocities and their violence can be visited on anybody that disagrees with them in any given situation."

The law and the Klan. They could become one and the same in that mounting orgy of violence. Listen to the story of three young civil rights workers—Michael Schwerner, Andrew Goodman, and James Chaney.

# 10

## TRIPLE EXECUTION

On June 21, 1964, the three young men disappeared in Mississippi.

Forty-four days later their bodies were found, decomposed, buried deep in an earthen dam.

Who were they? And why were they murdered?

Michael Schwerner, twenty-five years old that year, was a white social worker, born in New York. He had come to Mississippi early in 1964 because he felt he belonged there. "Nothing threatens peace among men like white supremacy," he once said. "Nowhere else in the world is the idea of white supremacy more firmly entrenched, or more cancerous, than in Mississippi. The Ku Klux are as much the victims of white supremacy as the Negroes are. So this is the decisive battleground for America, and every young American who wants to have a part in the decision should be here."

James Chaney, twenty-one and black, was born in Meridian, Mississippi. He had volunteered to join the staff of the civil rights movement in his native state.

Andrew Goodman, twenty-one, was a white student at Queens College, New York. He had come to Mississippi to help the movement during the summer months.

Michael Schwerner, with his wife Rita, had been working in Mississippi since January 1964. Placed in Meridian by the movement, their job was to build a community center, a sort of settlement house, that might appeal to blacks of all ages. The husband-and-wife team were well prepared for such a task. Michael had been trained in settlement house work and Rita to teach young children. There, in the local black schools, they found about fifty students ready to join the movement. (Among them was James Chaney.) Day after day groups of volunteers canvassed house-to-house, trying to persuade blacks to visit the Community Center, to try to qualify to vote, or to support the movement in some way.

For months they carried on their difficult work, making slow progress because, as Schwerner said, "Fear is holding the entire city back." The freedom workers knew they were hated by the whites. Yet for five months nothing happened to them beyond minor harassment. The reason, according to William Bradford Huie, the Southern reporter who wrote a book about it, was this:

> The smart way to resist "agitators" in Mississippi is not to break their heads but to protect them and let time and circumstance break their hearts. The men with the power in Mississippi know this. Only the peckerwood politicians and the jerks in the back-woods don't know it. This is why the prosperous, growing cities of Jackson, Meridian and Biloxi are relatively safe for "agitators"—and why most of the violence occurs in places like Philadelphia and McComb. Violence is bad business.... Had Schwerner remained in Lauderdale county and not ventured into the rural counties, he'd be alive today...."

But Schwerner wanted to expand his work into those outlying counties where life was much harder for blacks. The more persecution they felt, the more they were willing to risk for freedom. In the rural districts he found black adults ready to talk, ready to act, even in defiance of the sheriff and the Klan.

Chaney helped by scouting these counties in his car, seeking out rural blacks who might be persuaded to try to vote. Sometimes Schwerner went with him into Philadelphia, the county seat of Neshoba, about thirty-six miles from Meridian. Neshoba's sheriff, Lawrence Rainey, and his one deputy, Cecil Price, were close to the Klan. The sheriff had just won office by promising he would "handle the niggers and the outsiders."

Late that May, Schwerner and Chaney persuaded blacks in Longdale, a part of Neshoba County, to risk allowing a Freedom School to be conducted in their Mt. Zion Methodist Church. It would help prepare local people to qualify to vote. Soon after that decision Michael and Rita Schwerner drove north to Oxford, Ohio, where 300 volunteers were training to come to Mississippi for the Freedom Summer of 1964. The Schwerners were to help with the training and to choose one dedicated volunteer who would come back with them and work with Chaney in the Freedom School in Neshoba. Andrew Goodman was their choice. On June 20 he drove back to Mississippi with his new friends.

Neshoba County, said a Chamber of Commerce leaflet, "is a thriving community of over 21,000 friendly and hospitable people... A visitor to our community finds an old-fashioned welcome and a degree of friendliness that exists in no other place."

And it was a good place to live, wrote William Bradford Huie:

> If you are white and have a job and want simplicity. Most people who move there from the North like it. There is no traffic problem. Housing is cheap. Neither the air nor the streams are polluted. The hunting is excellent. Fish bite the year round. Taxes

are low. Weather is kind. Television reception is good. Competition is relaxed. Nobody is in a hurry. So if you are white and Christian and not a union organizer or a civil rights advocate, you may agree that Neshoba County is the friendliest place on earth.

Even if you are a Negro you may find it friendly—if you'll stay in your place. If you "talk like a nigger" and "act like a nigger." If you'll call all white men Mister. If you'll report for work on time, "work like a nigger" at your menial job, then get out of sight. But don't try to register to vote. Or use the public swimming pool or public golf course. Don't educate your son and try to get him a job as a fireman or a policeman. Don't educate your daughter and try to get her a job as a salesgirl or as a secretary at the courthouse. If you do something like that you'll reveal that you are an "agitator," and you better take the next bus to Chicago. You aren't being friendly. You are trying to make trouble and give the friendly community a bad image.

In the county seat of Philadelphia, besides the sheriff and his deputy, there were based several other officers of the law—city policemen, state highway patrolmen, auxiliary police and a National Guard unit. Some of them, it turned out, were members of the Klan, while others were tied to it by family, business, social or political connections.

Some or all of these officers may have known that white supremacy terrorists had met to adopt a master plan to protect their territory against "race mixers." On June 20, the day the Freedom Summer volunteers started from Ohio for Mississippi, the U.S. Senate passed a Civil Rights Bill. The next day Mississippi's front pages carried the response of Governor

Ross Barnett: "This action is repulsive to the American people. Turmoil, strife and bloodshed lie ahead."

What such leaders predict, white supremacy terrorists are likely to carry out. Already, in May, the terrorists had burned at least one cross in every Mississippi county—in Neshoba, twelve crosses at the same time in twelve different places, one of them on the courthouse lawn. Dozens of churches had been burned and even more homes dynamited. Many whippings had been given. And now, a white enemy—"the Jew-boy with the beard at Meridian"—was to be murdered. Huie estimates that at least two hundred men knew Michael Schwerner had been given a death sentence a month before his execution.

On Saturday night, June 20, Schwerner, Goodman and Chaney had reached Meridian after the long drive from Ohio and gone to sleep. The next morning they learned that the Longdale church had been burned down a few days before, and several black people had been beaten up. Schwerner decided to visit them for a few hours that afternoon, and took Jim Chaney and Andy Goodman with him—even though phone calls threatening him with death had come in to the Community Center.

They filled the station wagon's gas tank in Meridian and drove off, Chaney at the wheel, the two others beside him in the front seat. They reached Longdale about 1 P.M. They inspected the ruined church, then visited with the black families who told them what had happened and said the whites who did it were looking for Schwerner.

On the way back they were arrested by Deputy Price for "investigation" and driven to the county jail in Philadelphia. They were locked up and forbidden to use the phone. While the three sat in jail, the terrorist conspirators planned how to carry out Schwerner's execution. They wanted him alone, but they decided to kill the other two because they couldn't figure out how to let them go without their knowing too much. They argued a long time over who would have the honor of pulling the trigger on "the two Jews and the coon."

When the three did not show up in Meridian by 4 P.M., the alarm went out that they were missing. At 10:30 P.M. the three were released from jail, got into their station wagon and drove down the highway past a point where the conspirators waited. Soon they saw cars pursuing them and speeded up to evade them. But Deputy Price's car came up with siren screaming and red lights flashing and signaled them to stop. They were taken out of the station wagon and carried off four miles. They were then stood up by the road, and shot dead. Schwerner first, then Goodman, and then Chaney.

The bodies were thrown into the station wagon and driven to a farm near Philadelphia where a pond was under construction. Using a bulldozer, the killers buried the three young men, side by side, face down, deep in the earthen dam. Then they drove the station wagon fifteen miles to the opposite side of Philadelphia, on the edge of a swamp, doused it with diesel fuel, and burned it.

Everyone knew the missing men would not be traced by local authorities. The federal government stepped in, using an old law against conspiracy passed in 1870 to curb the Klan of Reconstruction days. The charred station wagon was found two days after the murder by Indians from the nearby Choctaw reservation. President Johnson ordered four hundred sailors from a nearby naval air base to join the FBI in the search for the missing men. Forty-four days after their disappearance, with clues from informers, the FBI found their bodies in the dam.

In December 1964, twenty-one men were arrested for conspiracy to violate the civil rights of the three freedom workers. Six were identified by the FBI as members of the White Knights of the Klan. A local grand jury refused to indict. And the state did nothing, either.

It took the federal government three years to get indictments and a trial under the Conspiracy Act of 1870. In 1967, a white jury heard the case. Three Klansmen who took part in the conspiracy confessed. None of the defendants took the stand. Nine of them were identified as Klansmen by informers who told of the meeting which ordered the "elimination" of Michael Schwerner. (Half the men who planned the murder had been shown the movie *Birth of a Nation* by Klan organizers within the preceding year.)

The jury reached a verdict: Klan Wizard Sam Bowers, Deputy Sheriff Cecil Price and five other Klansmen were found guilty. They were sent to prison for from three to ten years, with parole possible earlier. By 1976 most of them were free.

# 11

## A LIST

The Kluxers of the 1980s are younger. Usually they are in their twenties and early thirties, wearing their hair in the current style, sporting clothes to suit the fashion. When their leaders go on TV talk shows, they dress like respectable businessmen and sound calm and reasonable. But at their rallies they still wear white robes and hoods, burn crosses and rant against the blacks and the Jews. They spill the same racist garbage their grandfathers did in the 1920s when the Klan enrolled millions of members and was a power in politics.

Today's Klan is much smaller—maybe 10,000 members, according to Klan-watchers. But in recent years the KKK has steadily increased its non-member sympathizers, and its tactics have become more violent. It seeks confrontation wherever community tensions and civil disorders give it an opening. Year after year, the Justice Department records Klan-connected incidents of violence and terror on a rising curve. Cross-burnings, beatings, whippings, shooting, fire-bombings are common.

Look at this list, taken from press reports. It's a long one, but it will help you see what's going on. Details are left out. Only the essential facts are given:

1977—SAN DIEGO, CA: Two Klansmen are charged with

shooting at the home of one Chicano family and with conspiracy to shoot at another.

1977—OKLAHOMA CITY, OK: Members of a high school Ku Klux Klan chapter take credit for baseball bat attacks on patrons of a gay club.

1977—LOS ANGELES, CA: Three Klansmen convicted of conspiracy to murder the West Coast leader of the Jewish Defense League.

1977—ST. LOUIS, MO: Klansmen carrying signs saying "Down with ERA and NOW" picket the state International Women's Year Conference. The head of the United Klans of America says his "ladies' auxiliary" is working to oppose the women's movement, which he says was "trying to destroy all the principles and heritage that I cherish."

1978—JACKSON, MS: A fiery cross destroys the electrical supply for a newspaper that ran articles exposing the Governor's appointment of Klansmen to high office. A note on a brick that broke the newspaper's window said, "You are being watched by the Ku Klux Klan."

1978—ATLANTIC CITY, NJ: Two Klansmen hang a rabbi in effigy, in a public park.

1978—CULLMAN, AL: The Klan admits involvement in the kidnapping and beating of a black minister by three carloads of whites.

1979—CLINTON, TN: A Klansman is charged with murdering a white woman by setting her house afire because her sister was married to a black man and black friends visited the house.

1979—SYLACAUGA, AL: A Klansman is convicted of whipping a white woman who he thought was dating a black man.

1979—DECATUR, AL: Two hundred armed Klansmen mob a supermarket being picketed by two blacks. Police officers stand by as Klansmen wrap a Confederate flag around one black and set the other's hat on fire. A black shopper is knocked into his car and Klansmen fire on a black passerby. The only arrests are the two pickets, charged with "obstructing a business."

1979—DECATUR, AL: After the City Council passes a law banning guns at public rallies, 150 Klansmen, openly displaying guns, ride through town running stop lights, while police watch. They drive to the mayor's house with signs reading, "If You Want Our Guns, You Come and Get Them."

1979—DECATUR, AL: Eighty heavily armed Klansmen attack a group of black marchers who are protesting the rape conviction of a retarded black man.

1979—SAN DIEGO, CA: Two Klansmen are found guilty of killing a fellow Klansman they suspect had informed police about drug dealing by Klan members.

1979—TRENTON, NJ: A group of Klansmen vandalize a synagogue.

1979—NEW HAVEN, CT: A cross is burned in front of an office of the State Treasurer, the state's highest-ranking black official.

1979—DENVER, CO: Twenty Klansmen mount a picket line in front of a synagogue, shouting racist slogans. Some stores are plastered with stickers urging boycott of Jewish merchants.

1979—MUSCLE SHOALS, AL: Two Ku Klux Klansmen are charged with attacking two black ministers at a restaurant.

1979—TALLADEGA COUNTY, AL: Nine Klansmen are convicted of racial terrorism. They had flogged a white man who had black visitors in his home, and had shot into homes of black leaders and racially mixed couples.

1980—BIRMINGHAM, AL: A Klansman is convicted of violating the civil rights of two Vietnamese refugees. He had warned them to leave their jobs and had threatened to kill them if they told anyone.

1980—DALLAS, TX: Because a white truck driver stopped the rape of a black woman by three white men, Klansmen vandalize his car and engage him in many fights. He has had to move three times and now carries a gun for self-protection.

1980—BARNEGAT TOWNSHIP, NJ: A Ku Klux Klan leader and two sympathizers plead guilty to shooting at the home of a black family.

1980—HOPEWELL, VA: Black residents of a housing subdivision report a cross-burning rally of robed Klansmen.

1980—LAS VEGAS, NV: A threatening telephone call to actor Redd Foxx by a caller claiming to be a Klansman is followed up by the splashing of red paint on the comedian's house, along with the initials "KKK."

1980—CHATTANOOGA, TN: Three Klansmen shoot and wound four black women who are walking down a street. Earlier, the Klansmen had burned two crosses.

1980—FT. CHAFFEE, AK: The Ku Klux Klan holds two anti-Cuban rallies in the area where Cuban refugees are housed.

1980—FONTANA, CA: A black employee of the Pacific Telephone Co. is shot while working in a lift-bucket above a telephone pole, just two hours before a Klan rally. The assailant shouts a racial slur. A cross had been burned in the black man's yard a few months earlier.

1980—CHICAGO, IL: A man in a white sheet places a flaming cross in the yard of a two-family house occupied by a black family and a Latino family.

1980—CHATTANOOGA, TN: Three Klansmen armed with bombs, a bow and steel-tipped arrows, are arrested after a high-speed chase from a black neighborhood. They had been spotted near where four black women were gunned down by Klansmen in April.

1980—DETROIT, MI: Four Klansmen fire a shotgun at a black man and fire into his home. They had also planned to burn another black family's home in a suburb.

1980—HALTOM CITY, TX: About twenty robed Klansmen demonstrate outside a City Council meeting against 138 Cuban refugees brought there to work in the construction industry.

1980—GREENSBORO, NC: An all-white jury acquits four Klansmen and two Nazis who had been charged with killing five people at an anti-Klan demonstration in November 1979. The head of the American Nazi Party calls the verdict "a great victory for white America."

1980—HOUSTON, TX: A Ku Klux Klansman and a convicted felon teach Boy Scouts and Civil Air Patrol cadets how to strangle people, decapitate people with a machete, and fire semi-automatic weapons. The two men make racial slurs about blacks. In addition, the Klansman is quoted as saying: "There are only two groups I'll battle with, Communists and homosexuals. That's the basic reason I joined the Klan."

1980—GREAT NECK, NY: Students in this predominantly Jewish community arrive at high school to find spray-painted swastikas, obscenities, and a five-foot-high "KKK." This area has witnessed a rash of cross-burnings and anti-Semitic vandalism over the last year.

1980—BAYSIDE, QUEENS, NY: A man dressed in a Ku Klux Klan outfit burns a cross in front of the Jewish Center and synagogue.

1980—FRANKLIN, TN: A Klansman is arrested at a Klan roadblock on charges of illegal possession of a firearm.

1981—SAN LEANDRO, CA: Crosses are burned in front of two homes. One belongs to an interracial couple. "KKK" is spray-painted on a garage door, a sledge hammer is thrown through a front window, and a note containing racial slurs and signed "The KKK" is left on a doorstep.

1981—SANTA FE, TX: Klansmen armed with 30–30 hunting rifles and AK-47 semi-automatic rifles burn a twenty-five foot cross to protest Vietnamese refugee fisherman in the area.

1981—MEMPHIS, TN: Two Klansmen abduct a man who quit the Klan. They threaten him with a pistol, then cover him with yellow paint and feathers. Police learned that a "contract" was issued on his life because he publicly claimed that Klan leaders were selling marijuana and cocaine, and that a member had recruited women for porno movies.

1981—SALT LAKE CITY, UT: A former Klansman is convicted of killing two black men (eighteen and twenty year-olds) who were jogging with two white women in August 1980.

1981—BALTIMORE, MD: The leader of the Maryland Knights of the Ku Klux Klan is convicted of plotting to bomb a synagogue. A former police officer, he is also convicted of throwing a brick through the synagogue window.

1981—WILMINGTON, DE: Klan members and sympathizers are arrested on charges of plotting bombing of Baltimore office of NAACP, burning crosses in black neighborhoods, and violating weapons laws.

1981—NASHVILLE, TN: Klansmen are arrested for plotting bombing of a Jewish temple, a television tower and several Jewish-owned businesses.

1981—CATONSVILLE, MD: Klansmen are sentenced to eight years in prison for conspiring to bomb a local synagogue.

1981—SACRAMENTO, CA: A blitz of anti-Vietnamese hate mail signed "KKK" stuns refugee community and some families flee the city in fear.

1981—NEW ORLEANS, LA: Seven Klansmen and Nazis are convicted of violating U.S. neutrality laws in an aborted plot to take over the government of Dominica, a Caribbean island, and are sentenced to three-year prison terms.

1981—DETROIT, MI: Three Klansmen are indicted for conspiracy to murder a black man because he lived with a white woman.

1981—CEDARTOWN, GA: The Klan threatens and harasses Hispanic workers at a meat-packing plant.

1981—UNIONTOWN, PA: A Klan Kleagle is charged with the murder of a sixty-eight-year-old black man.

This list is selective. It could have been much longer. Proof enough, as it is, of how widespread Klan action is in our time. Let's examine some special aspects of the Klan—its interest in young people, to begin with.

# 12

# THE YOUNG
# COME FIRST

Did you notice the second item on the long list in the previous chapter? Members of a high school Ku Klux Klan chapter went into a gay club in Oklahoma City and attacked the patrons with baseball bats. Today the Klan is out to recruit young people. In many cities across the country it has passed out leaflets to high school students asking: "Are you fed up to here with black, Chicano and Oriental criminals who break into your lockers and steal your wallets and clothes?" If you are, the leaflet says, join the Klan Youth Corps and do something about it.

The appeal to youth has not recruited them in great numbers. But the Klan keeps at it, and its efforts are a real danger. Each of the so-called "national" Klans has tried to organize young people into a Klan Youth Corps or a Junior Klan. The Klan leaders say their aim is simply to teach children "ethical and moral values" and to give them "a basic knowledge of patriotism and the family unit."

The leaflets go beyond that. One handed out near schools says this:

An attempt is being made...to undermine young people's respect for the values of our nation and race. Black studies glorify mythological achievements of the black race. Christian values have been replaced by Jewish history... Jewish publishing houses have complete control over the editing, production and writing of the nation's textbooks... Little notice is given to the violence against students by the black savages who roam the corridors at will. Murder of white students by black students is on the increase.

Klan Youth Corps meetings open with the Pledge of Allegiance, just as in many classrooms. But instead of reading, writing and arithmetic, the children are taught white superiority and to beware the enemy—the Jew and the black. The young people are told that they are losing all their rights to minorities. One leaflet ticks off the Youth Corps program:

- Organize white youth in every school along white lines.
- Get tough with arrogant non-whites.
- Demand segregation of classes, followed by segregation of schools.
- Boycott school administrators who "appease" blacks.

In Texas, Ohio, California, Alabama, Louisiana, Colorado, Illinois, Indiana, and Oklahoma young people wear Klan T-shirts and take part in Klan survival courses and para-military training. "Open the portal of the world," they chant, "and go your way as Klan youth ready to die." Although Klan leaders have boasted of having youth corps in every state, observers believe they exaggerate mightily. Reporters visiting Klan youth camps find most of the children are there because their parents are Kluxers.

Jerry Thompson spent more than a year as an undercover investigator within the Klan. In an article he wrote after he surfaced, he said:

I was saddened every time I saw Klan children at a KKK function. In the flickering light of huge crosses in vacant fields there were always the beautiful, shining faces of small children—boys and girls—not yet in their teens: Klan children. They are being indoctrinated with the Klan's racist doctrine of white supremacy. Each time I saw them I felt sorry for them. And then, there was a Sunday afternoon, during a march of the Knights of the KKK through the streets of Birmingham when, suddenly, in the midst of two dozen Klan people wearing robes and hoods, there appeared this pretty girl, striding along fully robed and hooded, her lovely face reminding me of my own nine-year-old daughter. Her left arm was in a cast. Her eyes looked straight ahead. She was expressionless. I have no idea what she was thinking. Our Klan people kept referring to her as "cute." Seeing her made me want to cry.

In an editorial, the *Tennessean* warned of the "long-term threat of the virulent racism which the Klan spreads. This is seen most graphically and sadly in the faces of the Klan children, the sons and daughters of Klan members. As babies they are swaddled in the robes of the Klan, as children they are paraded in the Klan marches, as teen-agers they are inducted into the Klan Youth Corps and *taught* to hate—and so as adults they are misshapen in the image of the Klan."

There are many current examples of how the Klan draws in youth and what it does with them or through them. Here is a sampling:

- In Fontana, CA, a Klanswoman, wife of the state's Grand Dragon, leads a sixteen-member Brownie troop of the Girls Scouts.

- In Shelton, CT, the state's Grand Dragon is dismissed as a Boy Scout leader when his Klan involvement becomes public.
- In Marin County, CA, nine members of a high school football team are suspended after inserting "K-K-K" into a school cheer. Gym lockers have been marked "K-K-K."
- In Decatur, AL, members of the Klan Youth Corps burn a school bus at an anti-busing rally.
- In Franklin, TN, robed Klansmen ride school buses.
- In Birmingham, AL, the Klan places a large newspaper ad describing the schools as "jungles."
- In Durham, NC, a cross is burned at half-time during a game between black and white schools.
- In Chicago, IL, a high school teacher calling himself a "card-carrying member of the Klan" resigns when black students reveal he called them "little niggers," "bitches" and "prostitutes."
- In San Diego, CA, the Klan mails copies of *The White Student*, a white supremacy newspaper, to all members of the county's high school senior classes.

Children attending a Klan Youth Corps camp near Warrior, Alabama, in the summer of 1980 were interviewed by CBS-TV. Randy, a thirteen-year-old boy, was asked what the Klan meant to him. He said: "It stands for white supremacy. You know, to fight the Communists, to fight the niggers, and the Jews, and the Vietnamese, and everybody, you know, the Jews and Communists in America, and it means white supremacy."

Then, asked whether he thought it right for a young person to be taught to think about killing another human being, he replied: "We're out there because the civil war's coming, you know, there's another war coming. It's going to break out, and it's not going to stop until the last person's dead,

*A group of recruits at a Klan youth camp near Cullman, Alabama, listens to a lecture by Bill Wilkinson, Imperial Wizard of the Invisible Empire of the Knights of the KKK. In 1981 such camps offering paramilitary training were springing up in many parts of the country.*

and the kids are going to have to be tough, because we're the future Klan."

How tough, Imperial Wizard Bill Wilkinson made clear: "We're drumming into the Youth Corps that there are other uses for baseball bats than hitting home runs."

Pursuing young people a step beyond high school, the Klan has succeeded in recruiting groups of servicemen in the Army, Navy, Marine Corps and Air Force. Back in 1976, when racial violence broke out at a Marine Corps base in Camp Pendleton, California, it was discovered that white marines involved were members of the KKK. A Congressional inquiry was requested but it never came off.

Later in the 1970s, Klan groups surfaced in the Army and Navy. Soldiers at Fort Hood, Texas, and Fort Carson, Colorado, openly identified themselves as Klansmen and took part publicly in Klan activity. Dressed in army fatigues, some stood guard for the Klan at rallies in Texas and Louisiana.

Several ships of the Navy have also seen signs of KKK recruitment. When the supply ship *Concord* experienced several racial clashes, about twenty Klansmen were found to be aboard and some of them were transferred. On the aircraft carrier *Independence*, three white sailors put on Klan robes and confronted black shipmates. Aboard another carrier, the *America*, a cross-burning was reported. On the submarine tender *Canopus*, several sailors were reported to be signing up Klan members. Three of them were transferred or dismissed. The Navy issued an order to all ship and shore commanders to crack down on "racist activity."

Navy officials pointed out that no federal or military law prohibits KKK membership. But Admiral Harry D. Train II, commander of the Navy's Atlantic fleet, added:

> Overt or covert behavior which advocates the superi-
> ority of one race or ethnic group over another is

> disruptive to good order and discipline and will not
> be tolerated ... When there is public advocacy of
> racial or ethnic intolerance in our units, proselytiza-
> tion for membership in segregated organizations or
> the distribution of inflammatory material, such be-
> havior is contrary to good order and discipline.

In 1981, a German newsmagazine, *Stern*, charged that a U.S. Air Force staff sergeant had been recruiting Nazis to the Klan. Sgt. Murray Kachel admitted to the reporter that he was recruiting Germans to build "a second front" for the Klan in Europe. He said: "Not only the nigger, but the Jew is our enemy. We are facing a new race war and have to be prepared for it. The white race must return to its old greatness. You Germans have a long racially conscious tradition. Even the Americans can learn something from it."

That was only one sign of sharply increased KKK activity at almost all Army, Navy, and Air Force commands in Europe, according to a report made to the Department of Defense in 1981. On every base or post visited, researchers reported finding Klan literature and membership cards, sheets, mark-ings on walls or cross-burnings. The investigators said the military seemed to be doing little or nothing to deal with the nature or extent of KKK activity. The Klan seemed to attract the American "heirs of Hitler" in West Germany especially. It was estimated that several thousand of the 200,000 military personnel stationed there might be Klan members.

# 13

## WHO JOINS, AND WHY

What kind of people join the Klan? What makes some men and women respond to its appeal?

There is no simple answer. We are all different from one another in too many ways for any formula to account for our individual behavior. The human personality is complex and even mysterious. Two people raised in the same family, with the same education and opportunities, can make very different choices in life. Their paths may go in opposite directions. One may end up committing armed robbery, while the other becomes a labor organizer. Or one may become a teacher and the other a Kluxer.

Still, even if you cannot explain the behavior of particular people, it is possible to draw certain conclusions about the behavior of groups of people. Historians, sociologists, social psychologists study the actions of people in groups or classes and over periods of time. Often they can offer us some useful clues as to why such groups tend to act in certain ways.

In the case of the Ku Klux Klan we've seen how central white supremacy is in their beliefs. All through the Klan's history, from 1865 down to today, race hatred has fired the emotions of Kluxers and led them to commit countless acts of violence. That hatred has most often been directed against non-white people or against ethnic groups the Klan believes are

*Opposing the rights of Vietnamese immigrants
to make a living fishing in Galveston Bay, the
Texas Klan threatened violence and burned a
fishing boat in a futile effort to frighten them off.*

inferior. Klan leaders have always held that American civilization is really Anglo-Saxon or Nordic at root. The only "true Americans" are white Anglo-Saxon Protestants. They claim that all others are alien and inferior peoples. These "inferiors"—Blacks, Jews, Catholics, Hispanics, Asians, Native Americans—the Klan tries to keep out of the country, and if they are here already, seeks to hold them down to the lowest rung on the ladder. Being on top—that's a primary prejudice. The Klan finds it easy to sell people on the idea that they are better than anyone else.

Two Southern reporters who knew many Klansmen described what makes them tick. Writing in the *Saturday Evening Post*, Kenneth Fairly and Harold Martin said:

> Deep angers and frustrations now motivate the Klansman. He is rebelling against his own ignorance, ignorance that restricts him to the hard and poorly paid jobs that are becoming scarcer every day. He is angered by the knowledge that the world is passing him by, that he is sinking lower and lower in the social order. The Negro is his scapegoat, for he knows that so long as the Negro can be kept "in his place," there will be somebody on the social and economic scale who is lower than he is. In the Klavern, in his robes, repeating the ancient ritual, he finds the status that is denied him on the outside.

But race prejudice is used for reasons beyond a gain in status for some people. It helps make easier the economic and political exploitation of its victims. By forcing blacks to work at menial jobs and for low wages, employers make more profit. By intimidating blacks from voting, whites ensure the election of their own candidates. The agitator who stirs up hatred toward other ethnic groups is an exploiter. He uses prejudice to win advantage for himself or his group.

Flag-waving pageantry, a sense of belonging, excitement, all add to the Klan's attraction. And, as always in the past, today the KKK draws its members and sympathizers from a minority of people who are badly upset by great changes in the world they live in.

In the 1980s, Americans are deeply disturbed by inflation, unemployment, the threat of nuclear war. They are concerned with public issues such as crime, welfare, busing, affirmative action programs, taxation. Over the past twenty years, public opinion and the laws have changed on many controversial issues such as civil rights and race relations. A sizeable minority of Americans find it hard to accept such deep change and bitterly resent it. Klan leaders play cleverly on this feeling. They insist it was better in the "good old days." They urge America to turn the clock back to the peaceful ways they imagine we once enjoyed. Wherever problems and conflicts exist, there are fertile grounds for the Klan and other extremists.

The Klan seizes upon such troubles and distorts or exploits them to draw into action the many Americans who feel "all at sea" about today's issues and are looking for easy answers. The Klan appeals to deep-seated prejudice and plants its propaganda in receptive minds.

How does it do that? Take the Pennsylvania steel towns of Pittsburgh and Youngstown. When several steel mills were closed in 1980, the Klan claimed affirmative action policies were hurting "real Americans" (meaning whites) looking for jobs. By blaming blacks for the community's troubles, the Klan hoped to win supporters for its white supremacy program.

In Meriden, Connecticut, the Klan found an issue during the spring of 1981. There was public protest over the shooting death of a black man suspected of shoplifting, by a policeman.

The Klan held a demonstration in support of the police that ended in a violent brawl with anti-Klan demonstrators.

That was standard operating procedure for the KKK. It spotted a controversial issue with racial implications, staged a demonstration in full Klan regalia, and delivered the usual racist speeches, hoping for the violence it got. The result was big news coverage locally and nationally, which spread the false notion that the Klan stands for "law and order."

Always news to editors, the Klan thrives on publicity. The press is on the lookout for sensational stories because they sell papers. And the Klan is happy to supply such news, even news you might think would turn readers off the Klan. But to the KKK, any mention is good news. In Chalmers' detailed study of the Klan he noted that, "in total, the American press was bold, cautious, cowardly, sensationalistic, partisan, conscientious, and heroic when it came to reporting the Klan. On the whole, the press explained it partially and poorly, and often not at all."

In the Klan's first appearance, during Reconstruction, the press was at first divided or uncertain about how to report it. But when the Southern Democratic newspapers saw its political direction, they mobilized public opinion behind the white supremacists and told how to join and build the KKK. The truth about the Klan was smothered. The Southern Republican papers were of course opposed to the Klan. But they proved too weak to withstand economic and physical pressures and collapsed as Reconstruction was overthrown.

In the 1920s, five newspapers won the Pulitzer Prize for their reporting of the Klan. In the past twenty years, several papers and magazines have given the Klan far more than routine coverage. *Time, Newsweek, Playboy,* the *New York Times,* the Nashville *Tennessean,* the Associated Press have all tried to expose the Klan. Their stories, unfortunately, sometimes serve the Klan's purpose. They report the Klan's racist views without bothering to contradict them. And readers write in to ask how they can join. Such articles often refer to the Klan's violence, but do not document it. The press ought never to take for granted that readers see through the Klan.

All too often, the media let the Klan dictate the news. Hungry for stories, the editors order coverage of "media events" the Klan cooks up for no other purpose than to obtain headlines. The Klan leader David Duke was especially clever in his manipulation of the media. Once, in 1977, he announced that a thousand Klansmen would undertake a "watch" along the Mexican border to aid the understaffed U.S. Border Patrol in stopping nightly crossings by illegal aliens. The press, TV and the national wire services took him seriously and gave it a big buildup. On the appointed night, three dozen cameramen and reporters showed up to observe the Klan's "border patrol"—and found eight Kluxers there. But the media had given the Klan the headlines it wanted. Duke handled TV talk shows in the same way, making a favorable impression on many of them because the interviewers were too ill-prepared to ask the right questions.

In Michigan, a Klansman told a reporter the local Klavern met weekly with fifty members present. The press ran the story, with followup items handed them by the Kluxers for five weeks running. The Klansman was invited twice to speak to hundreds of students in the local high school. The press helped convince the public that the Klan was an important local organization— until belated investigation proved the Klan "leader" was the only Kluxer in town.

An expert at playing tricks with the press was Jeff Murray, former Klan leader. He told the *Columbia Journalism Review*: "We used the press. We lied and did anything we could to make reporters happy. We intentionally staged things just to get coverage." He said he called press conferences to hand out his lies. "I'd always get the same standard questions. Almost every reporter asks the same thing, almost like they're robots or something. They always want to know how many members we have, what the cross-burning means, how are we organizing. We always gave 'em good answers." By good, he meant lies that built the Klan to far more than its real strength. If reporters would research the necessary background first, and never take the Klan quotes at their face value, they would provide readers with more accurate stories.

The job of the news media should be to make every effort to investigate all aspects of the Klan thoroughly. Some argue that the Klan gets too much publicity. Too much if it is glib and superficial. Never enough if it is honest and probing. The media do have an obligation to report "hard news." What the Klan does, no matter how offensive, should be reported. To ignore such stories would be to fail to inform the public that the Klan is active.

Stories that glorify the Klan appear here and there and are deplorable. *Esquire* printed an article painting the Klan as a bunch of patriotic Good Ole Boys. *The New York Times* ran some "Op Ed" page pieces sentimentalizing Klan members. Stories that are not real news and put the Klan in a favorable light make readers think the Klan is made up of harmless people with good intentions. The truth is it is made up of racists with a long history of violence.

# 14

## WHAT TO DO

What can be done about the Klan?

If we agree that bigotry and violence are harmful to the community, is there any way to combat them? Each of us has to make his or her own decision when confronted personally with racism and the violence it breeds. It is the responsibility of the community itself, however, to plan for and meet any crisis an organized movement like the Klan creates.

What course of action is best? There is no universal agreement, even among those, the great majority, who detest what the Klan stands for. Local responses to Klan actions show how differently various groups react. Some choose silence: better to ignore the Klan, give it no publicity, let its parades and speeches and demonstrations have their moments and disappear. Others do the extreme opposite: they organize counter-demonstrations, carry clubs and rocks and bottles and even guns, ready to use them.

The debate over the best way to meet bigotry and violence persists in private and in the press. The Klan has the same First Amendment right to express its views as other citizens. Free speech, free press and free assembly are rights guaranteed to all, protected by the Constitution and the courts. Upholders of the First Amendment believe the government should maintain a strict hands-off policy, no matter how offensive or emotionally distressing speech or communication may be. What may offend you may be what pleases another. Who is to decide what speech should be censored or silenced? Will the left suppress all right-wing opinions today? And the right suppress all left-wing opinions tomorrow? Thomas Jefferson had an unflinching faith in the people's ability to decide right or wrong, if the First Amendment permitted them to hear all opinions. He saw the First Amendment as vital to the continuation of a free society.

It is when Klan talk turns into intimidation and terror, when Klan actions violate basic rights, that the community must invoke existing laws against such illegal activity.

But where draw the line between opinion and action? In recent years, as anti-black and anti-Semitic acts have multiplied, there have been renewed demands for the outlawing of such groups as the Klan and the American Nazis. In California, a bill was introduced in 1981 to ban groups that teach and advocate violence. Rather than safeguard the right to free expression of gatherings whose slogans proclaim "Lynch Niggers" or "Kill Jews," the police would be called upon to arrest the speakers.

That bill was opposed by the American Civil Liberties Union. Such a law, it said, might allow law enforcement officers to violate the constitutional guarantees of free speech and assembly. Measures aimed at combating terrorism could be transformed into programs to punish political dissent and to erode civil liberties. Other groups feared the bill could result in a revival of McCarthyism, with unpopular radical groups becoming the target.

Those favoring such a measure ask: "Which is the greater danger—the possible harassment of legitimate dissidents or the unchecked proliferation of such elements as the KKK or American Nazis?" In the present climate, they say, the second possibility appears to be the more serious threat.

*To protest Klan terror, blacks and whites in Jacksonville,
Florida, mount a counter-demonstration in 1982.*

Those opposing measures to outlaw peddlers of hate and violence hold that it isn't possible under the Constitution to forbid the existence of organizations like the Klan. Only overt acts by individuals—not organizations and opinions—are punishable. They also argue that such laws would not reform Kluxers anyhow. Their attitudes aren't affected by legislation. To that the reply is made that yes, it would be better to have the moral rebirth of a Klansman, but it is the duty of a democracy to control his power to incite hatred and violence.

Law can act not only to deter such people, but by becoming part of the social creed, it influences citizens who don't want to put themselves outside the limits of what their community accepts. Law as well as custom has the power to educate people and to shape their conduct. Law can be an instrument of education. "A democracy," such thinkers say, "by outlawing an admitted evil, aids in its eradication."

An authority on the subject of terrorism, Brian Michael Jenkins of the Rand Institute, warns that perhaps the most serious side effect of such violence in the United States is the threat to civil liberties it creates:

> Perhaps the greatest danger posed by terrorism and indeed, sometimes its intended effect, is that it creates an atmosphere of fear and alarm in which a frightened population will clamor for draconian measures, totalitarian solutions. Terrorism should be fought with even more democracy.... This involves tasks of public education, reassertion of basic moral values and democratic principles.

In any case, lawmakers have not ignored the Klan. There are several federal statutes that make illegal KKK efforts to violate other citizen's constitutional rights. Such actions are punishable as federal felonies. Many states also have laws against typical Klan conduct, such as wearing masks, or burning crosses, or posting swastikas on another's property, or desecrating religious institutions. Of course, if Kluxers violate state criminal laws against murder, assault, kidnapping, terroristic threats, they can be punished like anyone else who commits those crimes. Many cities and towns also have ordinances which can be used against lawless Klan acts.

In many states laws prohibit the formation of private armies, which would rule out the Klan's paramilitary training programs. Even where states have no such laws, the training is banned if the Klan uses illegal weapons, or if the training is part of a conspiracy to deny other people their constitutional rights. Klan threats of violence are also illegal under federal civil rights laws as well as many state laws.

So there is substantial federal and state protection against the Klan and similar racist groups prone to violence. These laws do not deny the Klan or its members their constitutional rights. They simply prevent the Klan from violating the rights of other people.

To help citizens who are the victims of racist violence or intimidation there are numbers of lawyers around the country ready to represent them without cost. Klanwatch, a project of the Southern Poverty Law Center, 1001 South Hull Street, Montgomery, Alabama, 36101, makes referrals to such attorneys.

Set up to monitor Klan activities, Klanwatch distributes a wide variety of information services—for schools, churches and clubs, for lawyers, for law enforcement agencies, for other anti-Klan groups.

There are many things a community can do to cope with the Klan. It is not only the Klan's immediate targets—the minorities—who should be concerned. Stopping the hate peddlers is vitally important to the entire community. Every citizen should stand together with the direct victims to isolate the bigots. Martin Niemoeller, the German pastor who spent eight years in Hitler's prisons, gave us a warning we can't ignore:

> In Germany, they came first for the Communists, and I didn't speak up because I wasn't a Communist.
>
> Then they came for the Jews, and I didn't speak up because I wasn't a Jew. Then they came for the Catholics, and I didn't speak up because I was a Protestant.
>
> And then they came for me, and by that time, no one was left to speak up.

That is the lesson history teaches. The racists count on community indifference to enable them to do their vicious work. The churches, the labor unions, business and professional groups, schools and colleges, the fraternal societies—all have a moral responsibility to express their concern. They can act in many ways. In December 1980, the American Baptist Convention adopted a resolution on the resurgence of the Klan which can serve as a model for action by all kinds of other groups:

> As we enter the decade of the 1980s, the mood of America is characterized by growing economic unrest, unemployment, rapid social change and a sense of impotency and futility. That mood is contributing to a resurgence of the Ku Klux Klan, or to a "new Klan" in the United States.
>
> Public opinion has encouraged the growth of the Klan and racism in general when it has sympathized with it or indirectly supported it by endorsing the attitude that America's minorities have "come too

far, too fast." Public tolerance has been demonstrated in recent months by voter acceptance of Klan political candidates, widespread distribution of printed material which accepts KKK actions and by the failure of the criminal justice system to investigate effectively and end Klan-related violence.

THEREFORE: In accordance with the American Baptist Policy statement on Human Rights which supports the right of all persons to be protected against discrimination and in light of its concern over the current manifestations of racism as evidenced in the resurgence of the Ku Klux Klan, the Board of National Ministries urges local congregations and individuals to:

1. Indicate publicly their opposition to the Klan by statement and action wherever the Klan appears;

2. Encourage politicians and governmental bodies to take active positions against the racism, terrorism and acts of violence fostered by the Klan;

3. Educate members, especially children, about the nature of the Klan and about the myths which it seeks to foster related to racial superiority;

4. Design and implement programs to educate people, especially children about the biblical imperatives for racial justice;

5. Take every opportunity afforded by the media to affirm our support of racial justice; and

6. Become actively involved in local and national efforts to achieve and assure racial justice.

We call upon the agencies and the leadership of the regional and national units of American Baptist Churches in the USA to:

1. Provide information materials and other forms of support to individuals and to congregations engaged in efforts to educate their members about the nature of the Klan and about racial justice;

2. Represent American Baptist Churches in ecumenical efforts to combat the Klan;

3. Encourage public media to use their resources to promote racial justice;

4. Commend those media which have carried out investigative reporting about the Klan and its activities; and

5. Express our repugnance for the philosophy and activities of the Klan through appropriate governmental and legal channels.

There are some opponents of the Klan who have confronted it with violent tactics. In California, Ohio, North Carolina, Alabama, Mississippi, Klan demonstrators have been countered by groups wading in with clubs, iron bars, bricks and bottles. From the record, it appears that the principal victims of such clashes have been the police. Trying to separate the contending forces, they have suffered injuries caused by both sides.

Do street brawls contribute anything useful to campaigns against the Klan? They give the Klan an alibi: we carry weapons, they say, only to protect ourselves. When left-wing extremists fight it out with right-wing extremists on the streets, democracy loses. In a speech to Yale students in the fall of 1981, the university's president, A. Bartlett Giamatti, criticized such "peddlers of coercion" on both sides for their assault on civil rights. In the atmosphere they create, he went on, it becomes possible to "keep two sets of books on civil liberties, two sets of standards that can be applied as one's ideology demands, rather than the single standard set forth by the Bill of Rights."

**The Klan Rides Again**

Meriden Klan rally brings hatred into the open

Klan Group in Alabama Training for 'Race War'

More Arrests Expected in Klan Plot

Boys Reported Learning to Shoot And Kill at a Klan Camp in Texas

Admiral bans racist activity as fleet tolerates legal KKK

Klan Inflames Gulf Fishi~ ~etween Whites and Vie

Klansmen Are Among 10 Indicted In Plot c~ ~aribbean Island Nation

Klansman Backs Survival C~ That Teach Warfare to C'

Four Black Women Wound~ ~hattanooga; Klansmen ~

Violent Klan Gr~

Klan Activities Described ~earing in Alabama

Klan's blueprint for revolution, takeover of nation is revealed

Some schools have held teach-ins on the Klan and its racist views and practices. Groups have set up special study task forces to gather information about the Klan and bring it to their members for discussion. Individuals have prepared resolutions against the Klan and introduced them for action to their organizations. Some have petitioned their mayor or governor to speak out publicly against the Klan. Others have developed coalitions within their communities to combat Klan propaganda and actions.

One of the most timely warnings about the Klan comes from Paul Simon, U.S. Congressman from Ohio. He wrote:

> The Klan is a small blot on the national horizon and by themselves are not that much to worry about. The danger of the minor resurgence of the Klan is not that their membership ranks will grow; emotionally mature adults will not join them. The danger is that the lies and distortions which they spread are not always identified with the Klan.
>
> If this nation should go through some really difficult economic times during the next few years— much more difficult than we are now experiencing, and that is possible—then there will be those who will look for scapegoats rather than constructive answers.
>
> All of us should know that the forces of negativism, those who appeal to fear and prejudice and ignorance, render a great disservice to their country.

# BIBLIOGRAPHY

This is not a complete list of the research materials used in the course of preparing this book. The files of contemporary newspapers and periodicals were an invaluable source, but only a number of selected items are listed. Indispensable for recent coverage of the Klan are the Klanwatch *Intelligence Report* and the National Anti-Klan Network Newsletter. I also made constant use of *The New York Times* and its Index. News periodicals and newsletters, such as the *Washington Spectator*, were of added value. I want to thank the Council on Interracial Books for Children for making available to me its extensive file of newspaper and magazine reports on the Klan.

## BOOKS AND ARTICLES

Alexander, Charles. *The KKK in the Southwest.* Lexington: University of Kentucky, 1965.

Allport, Gordon W. *The Nature of Prejudice.* Reading, PA: Addison-Wesley, 1979.

Braden, Anne. "The Ku Klux Klan Mentality: A Threat in the 1980s." *Freedomways*, Vol. 20, No. 1, First Quarter, 1980, 7–14.

Brown, Richard Maxwell, ed. *American Violence.* Englewood Cliffs, NJ: Prentice Hall, 1970.

Calbreath, Dean. "Kovering the Klan: How the Press Gets Tricked into Boosting the KKK." *Columbia Journalism Review*, March–April, 1981.

Chalmers, David M. *Hooded Americanism*. New York: Franklin Watts, 1976, 1980.

Current, Richard N., ed. *Reconstruction*. Englewood Cliffs, NJ: Prentice Hall, 1965.

Fisher, William H. *The Invisible Empire: A Bibliography of the Ku Klux Klan*. Metuchen, NJ: Scarecrow Press, 1980.

Franklin, John Hope. "Birth of a Nation—Propaganda as History." *The Massachusetts Review*, Autumn, 1979. Vol. XX, No. 3, 417–434.

Frost, Stanley. *The Challenge of the Klan*. New York: AMS Press, 1969.

Gerlach, Larry R. *Blazing Crosses in Zion: The Ku Klux Klan in Utah*. Hogan: Utah State University Press, 1982.

Goldberg, Robert A. *The Hooded Empire: The Ku Klux Klan in Colorado*. Urbana: University of Illinois Press, 1981.

Holmes, Fred R. *Prejudice and Discrimination*. Englewood Cliffs, NJ: Prentice Hall, 1970.

Huie, William Bradford. *Three Lives for Mississippi*. New York: WCC Books, 1964.

Ingalls, Robert P. *Hoods: The Story of the Ku Klux Klan*. New York: Putnam, 1979.

Jackson, Kenneth. *The KKK in the City: 1915–1930*. New York: Oxford University Press, 1967.

Kennedy, Stetson. *Southern Exposure*. New York: Doubleday, 1946.

Scott, John Anthony. "The Origins and Development of the Ku Klux Klan as a Badge of Slavery." New York: Center for Constitutional Rights, 1981.

Shenton, James, ed. *The Reconstruction*. New York: Putnam, 1963.

Sims, Patsy. *The Klan.* New York: Stein and Day, 1978.

*Southern Exposure*, "Mark of the Beast: Special Section on the Ku Klux Klan." Summer, 1980.

Sterling, Dorothy. *The Trouble They Seen: Black People Tell the Story of Reconstruction.* New York: Doubleday, 1976.

Syrkin, Marie. "It's Time for a Law." *Midstream*, May, 1981, 52–54.

Thompson, Jerry. "My Life with the Klan." Nashville *Tennessean*, Special Supplement, Dec., 1980.

*The Tennessean*, "The New Klan: White Racism in the 1980's." Nashville, Tennessee.

Trelease, Allen W. *White Terror: The KKK Conspiracy and Southern Reconstruction.* New York: Harper & Row, 1971.

Turner, John. *The Ku Klux Klan: A History of Racism and Violence.* Montgomery: Klanwatch, 1982.

Whitehead, Don. *Attack on Terror: The FBI Against the Ku Klux Klan in Mississippi.* New York: Funk and Wagnalls, 1980.

## DOCUMENTS AND REPORTS

Epstein, Benjamin R. and Arnold Foster. *Report on the Ku Klux Klan.* New York: Anti-Defamation League of B'nai B'rith, 1965.

*Facts.* Periodic information bulletins published by Anti-Defamation League, 1951–1981.

Galbraith, Ronald E. and Janet Eyler. *How Is It Possible? An Examination of the Ku Klux Klan.* Nashville: Nashville Panel, 1980.

*Klanwatch Intelligence Reports.* Published by Southern Poverty Law Center, Montgomery, Ala.

*Under the Hood: Report on the KKK in the Greater Los*

*Angeles Area.* Los Angeles City Commission on Human Relations, 1980.

U.S. House of Representatives. 1965–66. *Activities of the Ku Klux Klan Organizations in the United States.* Report in Parts I–V of hearings before the Committee on Un-American Activities. 89th Congress, 1st and 2nd sessions. U.S. Government Printing Office.

U.S. House of Representatives. Dec. 11, 1967. *The Present-Day Ku Klux Klan Movement.* A Report by the Committee on Un-American Activities. 94th Congress, 1st session. U.S. Government Printing Office.

U.S. House of Representatives. 1981. *Increasing Violence Against Minorities.* Report by Committee on the Judiciary. 96th Congress, 2nd session. U.S. Government Printing Office.

*Violence, the Ku Klux Klan and the Struggle for Equality.* Published by Connecticut Education Association, Council on Interracial Books for Children, and National Education Association, 1981.

# INDEX